T]

Pacaa Nova

J

The Pacaa Nova

Clash of Cultures on the Brazilian Frontier

Bernard von Graeve

broadview press

Cataloguing in Publication Data

von Graeve, Bernard, 1941-
    Pacaa Nova: clash of cultures on the Brazilian frontier

ISBN 0−921149−36−0

1. Pacaa Nova Indians − Social Life and Customs. 2. Pacaa Nova Indians −
Cultural Assimilation. 3. Indians of South America − Brazil − Social Life
and Customs. 4. Indians of South America − Brazil − Cultural Assimilation.
5. Acculturation − Brazil − Case Studies. I. Title.

F2520.1.P28V66   1989   981'.00498   C89-093686-2

broadview press   broadview press
P.O. Box 1243   421 Center St.
Peterborough, Ontario   Lewiston, NY
K9J 7H5   Canada   14092   USA

Printed and Bound in Canada

CONTENTS

ACKNOWLEDGEMENTS

This book began with fieldwork conducted in Brazil in 1969 and 1970. I have the Canada Council and Trent University to thank for the funds that made that research and later visits possible.

A host of people contributed to the enterprise through their help and intellectual stimulation. Though I am grateful to every one of them, limited space allows me to acknowledge only some by name.

I extend my thanks to Florestan Fernandes, Eduardo Galvão, Adela E. de Oliveira, and others at the Museu Paraense Emilio Goeldi in Belem for their encouragement, support, and hospitality. Roberto Cardoso de Oliveira, whom I unfortunately met only briefly, greatly influenced the direction of my investigation.

In Guajará Mirim I owe a special debt to Padre F. A. Bendoraitis, whose active support was essential to my work in the field as well as to the Prelacy of Guajará Mirim, and to Dom Roberto de Aruda, who gave generously of his time. I am also indebted to Mrs. Barbara Kern and Royal Taylor of the New Tribes Missions for their time and help.

In Sagarana both the administration of the mission and the Pacaa Nova exhibited great patience and showed me genuine hospitality. Their understanding and help made my stay there a pleasant one.

Robert Shirley, my thesis supervisor, R.W. Dunning, David Price, and Linda Hubbell provided me with comments, suggestions and constructive criticism. Valerie Tadda rendered the charts and maps at a time when her own work was pressing, and I am grateful to her for that. Finally, thanks go to my mother, who spent weeks going over my sloppy writing and producing the first of many drafts, and to Gabriella Carr-Rollitt, whose typing assistance and constant encouragement and comments pushed me to finally finish and submit the manuscript.

Introduction

Brazil, Friday, April 10. The hot, heavy humidity that had preceded the torrential downpour was beginning to lift as the sun and a light breeze bought some relief; it was 29C, the air was still palpable, and insects swarmed and buzzed and waged their incessant war against anything human or animal. I'm finally on the river and on my way. As I gaze out over the edge of my cotton hammock, I can see brown, naked children playing a short distance away. They are sitting in a sunken dugout at the edge of the river. The narrow path behind them leads to a tall thatched hut in a small clearing, surrounded by yellow and red flowers and partially shaded by the dark green foliage of a huge mango tree. The children stare briefly at me and resume their play.

My hammock was slung across the width of a covered barge that was lashed to the side of a small motor vessel powered by a large Yanmar diesel engine. The odd-looking contraption moved upriver at a steady three knots. The captain, a tall, robust man with a cheerful, mahogany countenance, seemed unperturbed by heat or insects. He was an experienced river man and knew every current, eddy and bend in the river; at that moment he hugged the shore where the current was weakest. This was my second day with Captain Raymundo. He was on his way to the Guaporé River and the Brazilian settlement of Principe da Beira. I would leave him that night to begin my field work at a mission post for the famous, or infamous, Pacaa Nova, who recently had killed a family of Brazilian rubber tappers. Raymundo was pleased to have me, a "doctor," as a passenger. He had taken a similar passenger before, in 1956 when Franz Caspar visited the Tupari Indians.

Except for the ubiquitous parrots and hawks, we saw little wildlife, and had only passed isolated peasant huts and three or four very small settlements. The Mamoré river at this point is about five hundred meters wide and carried almost no traffic. We passed several flat-bottomed river boats riding the faster current in the middle of the stream on their way downriver; they were filled with bellowing cattle and flew the Bolivian flag. Otherwise, the impression was one of isolation, of a natural pristine environment that had changed little in the last hundred years.

River traffic near the junction of the Rio Pacaas Novas and Rio Mamoré.

The junction of the Mamoré and Guaporé rivers was only two hundred kilometers from Guajará Mirim, our port of embarcation, but would take over thirty hours to reach. Behind the barge bobbed a fourteen-foot aluminum runabout borrowed from a Canadian priest stationed at the Bolivian port of Guayaramerin. It was fitted with a 7 1/2 HP Johnson motor purchased in Manáus. In the boat, under a rubber poncho, were trade goods and supplies: a 16-gauge shotgun, a hammock and mosquito net, a small medical kit with chloroquine, antibiotics, lomotil, aspirin, a radio and personal effects.

Towards midnight, as we neared the destination, Raymundo cut the engines and brought his vessel closer to the left shore. We shook hands; with a quizzical look in his eyes and a raised eyebrow he wished me the best of luck. I thanked him warmly for his hospitality and, with a show of confidence released my boat and was adrift. I wasn't too concerned; after all, I had been here before. The mission where I would spend the next nine months was only about half an hour away on an old channel of the river. But it was now the end of the rainy season and everything looked different. After some momentary indecision, I started my motor and plunged ahead. In the darkness none of the old landmarks were visible and I became increasingly nervous as half an hour passed with nothing familiar in sight. Suddenly, a light appeared dead ahead, and I made a grateful beeline for it. On the bank of the river stood three men: the one with the flashlight was Joaquim, who ran the dispensary; with him were two very sleepy Pacaa Nova.

Three years before, while working in Ottawa, I had become involved in a planned expedition to the jungle of South America to mark Canada's centennial celebrations. Like so many grand schemes, the proposal foundered for lack of funds. By that time, however, I had been accepted as a doctoral candidate at the University of Illinois, and I decided to push ahead with my part of the expedition and make the legal and logistical arrangements for an archaeological survey and excavation in the floodplains — the Llanos de Mojos of eastern Bolivia. A detailed ethno-history of the area (by William Denevan) had excited my interest and raised a host of questions whose answers could only be obtained through archaeological fieldwork.

I left for Bolivia in May, but travel in remote areas of Bolivia was not easy in 1967. Che Guevara and his guerrillas were operating in the south and foreigners were in general suspect. Contact with the area's German community and the help of the Maryknoll fathers enabled me to travel relatively unmolested, to visit some of the sites reported by Denevan, and to see some of the artifacts found near them.

While in Guajará Mirim, on the border of Bolivia/Brazil, I was introduced to a padre medico (a doctor priest) who had established a mission settlement for the recently contacted (1961-62) Pacaa Nova Indians. He was about to visit the mission, which was several days' travel up the Mamoré, and invited me along. It was a unique opportunity and I jumped at the chance.

The mission post was relatively isolated and closed to outsiders; I thought at the time what an opportunity it would be for someone to conduct a study of planned culture change. The recent contact meant that fresh cultural and historical data would still be available.

Anthropological fieldwork, unlike laboratory experiments, depends greatly on opportunity, the political climate, events, and people. When circumstances conspired against me in 1968 and I was unable to pursue my archaeological project, it was only natural that I would turn to the culture change study. In the summer of 1969 I returned to Brazil to arrange for more extended fieldwork at the mission. Armed with a recommendation from Charles Wagley and a letter from Florestan Fernandes, an eminent Brazilian sociologist who was in Toronto at the time, I travelled to Belém and contacted Dr. Eduardo Galvão at the Museu Paraense Emilio Goeldi. He graciously provided me with associate status in the Museu; I spent several immensely enjoyable and stimulating weeks in the library and in the company of Brazilian colleagues. On Dr. Galvão's recommendation I visited Roberto Cardoso de Oliveira in Rio de Janeiro. Although we met only briefly, he provided me with copies of his articles on internal colonialism and inter-ethnic friction — articles that were later to be very influential in reorienting my research.

In May, 1969, I arrived in the field for a three-month period. This first phase of field work proved to be discouraging, both in terms of my personal adaptation and role, and in terms of the very limited data I could collect. My beginners Portuguese was no doubt partially responsible for my difficulties, but much more serious was my total dependence on the staff of the mission. The padre medico, who did not himself live at the mission, had arranged for me to stay with the teacher, who apparently was given instructions to look after me. He even tried to help me elicit information from the Indians. I felt stifled and at the same time helpless, unable to disassociate myself from the mission. Collecting data also proved to be frustrating; the world of the Pacaa Nova seemed impenetrable. On more than one occasion, mothers used my approach to frighten their children into obedience by warning them that "wijam will get you." *Wijam* is the Pacaa Nova word for outsider, and in this case had the connotation of a bogey man.

Three months later, aside from some basic census data and mapping, I seemed to have achieved little of value. Completely discouraged, I left the field in August, unsure if I could accomplish anything or endure a longer stay.... .

But here, at midnight, this time with my own boat, motor, and shotgun, I was ready to try again. A hut had been built for me at the edge of the village through the kindness of the padre medico. It provided me with some independence and the physical separation from the mission staff that was vital if I was to collect any data. In the ethnically stratified environment of the mission, it would have been inadvisable for me to live with the Indians, nor would they have felt comfortable with an outsider among them. As things stood, my house was on the path to the gardens and was isolated enough so that they could visit me without being observed by the mission staff.

Rubber gatherers in Pacaa Nova territory.

Initially, I lived alone, but was a constant object of attention, especially by members of a group who had come into contact in January of 1969. They came to stare, to wonder at my beard and the hair on my body, to explore my possessions; they never tired of listening to my radio or just watching my strange behaviour and mysterious activities. When it became known that I also had a supply of trade goods, a regular procession carrying eggs, meat, sweet potatoes, arrows and feather ornaments came to my house with requests for knives, machetes, fishing hooks or line, and shotgun shells.

In late May, Pancabrem, a man of middle age, began to visit me quite regularly each morning. Unlike earlier visitors, he made no requests or demands. When I first invited him to eat with me he felt that he had to reciprocate by sweeping the floor of my hut. His offer of friendship seemed genuine; other members of the settlement began to refer to him jokingly as my "ate" or father. He had a reputation for not having much to do with outsiders, so his interest in me undoubtedly increased my standing and rapport with the Indians of the mission. During my stay at Sagarana, Pancabrem continued to be a loyal friend.

In June, Uruaunkun, the young husband of one of the first victims of a measles epidemic that had just swept the mission, asked to move in with me. He had worked in Guajará Mirim and spoke fluent Portuguese, and his presence in my house would give me some access to the gossip of the mission post. I cleared out the storage room for him and he stayed with me until my departure from the mission. As it turned out, I saw little of him at Sagarana, but he was invaluable to me as a guide on my trip to the settlements on the Rio Pacaas Novas.

My role at the mission was a puzzle to the Indians. The concept of research and study of other cultures held no meaning for them. All I could do was try to disassociate myself as much as possible from the local mission staff, although my presence depended to some extent on their goodwill and support. Despite their limited contact with civilizados (a term the non-natives use to distinguish themselves from the Indians), the Pacaa Nova had learned to differentiate several types of outsiders: members of the local population who ordered them about and did not hide their contempt for them, and those from further away, who came with presents, showed them more kindness, and who were treated with deference by the locals. The younger men who had worked in Guajará Mirim could distinguish two further categories among those bearing gifts — Brazilians and foreigners — and they knew that the Padre himself was one of the latter. My identification with the "tribe" of the padre undoubtedly raised my status, and accounts for the fact that Indians frequently came to me in the hope that I might intercede with him on their behalf.

Unlike the local staff, I did not criticize or show disgust or disapproval of Pacaa Nova culture, and my house was always open to them. They developed a special fascination for my tape-recorder. Whole groups of younger men and some women would gather to record songs or stories, or to listen to recordings of some social or ritual event.

My fieldwork was conducted in Portuguese, the language of the dominant society. Although this clearly limited the information that I could obtain about the culture of the Pacaa Nova, it proved more useful as my focus shifted to the mission and to the inter-ethnic situation. Since about a dozen of the younger men had worked in Guajará Mirim and attended school in Sagarana, they spoke sufficient Portuguese to serve as interpreters. I knew that they, more than others, would be most aware of local prejudices and disapproval of Indian culture, and would be tempted to distort or ignore answers to questions about sensitive topics. To guard against this, I had laboriously copied a two thousand-word draft dictionary of Portuguese-Pacaa Nova collected by the New Tribes missionaries. I also went over the extensive notes on native culture kept by the missionaries during the early years of contact while the culture still displayed some vigour. The data had originally been collected to facilitate Bible translation, a task that required detailed knowledge of cultural, especially religious, concepts. Since religion is thoroughly integrated with the rest of culture, their observations proved invaluable; they described elements of culture that had been put aside and did not emerge from my interviews. At the time of my fieldwork, the Pacaa Nova were very evasive about their past practices, and were sensitive to the reactions of Brazilians. Their reluctance to talk about their culture was part of their adaptation to the new situation.These notes allowed me to pursue topics that would otherwise have been overlooked or lost.

My attempts to gather information were further complicated by the mission staff's genuine desire to assist me. Their idea of data collecting was to summon the informant and demand information; when this was not forthcoming they lost patience, and the whole episode merely strengthened their conviction that Indians are irrational. The younger men denied their culture most vehemently and insisted that they no longer followed "the way of the forest". They were, in fact, so circumspect that the overseer of the mission, who had lived in very close quarters with them, was convinced that they did not even talk about many of the things that had been done in the past. He told me that they had a "different language" for these things, one he did not understand. This denial of traditional culture made it very difficult for me in the early period, when, armed with concepts of descent, locality and alliance, I attempted to discover their "system" and to collect some of the traditional ethnographic information. Kinship and residence rules were especially difficult to reconstruct, since the Pacaa Nova had lost over seventy-five percent of their population in the first year of contact. The epidemics had broken up families, wiped out whole groups, disrupted preferential marriages and caused general chaos. All of this was aggravated by the congregation of the various remnant groups at Indian Service and mission posts. It was within the context of these artificial settlements that they were now attempting to reconstruct a viable social system and find a new basis for cooperation and co-residence.

As I spent more time at the mission, I became aware that what I was observing was not the restructuring of an independent or semi-independent social group, but rather a group whose choices and decisions were being dictated to by the outside, or by the nature of contact with the outside.

I entered the field with a variety of preconceptions and expectations about change based on the concept of culture and acculturation, and found these inadequate. I wanted to understand the contemporary condition of the Pacaa Nova in its broadest context. It became increasingly clear to me that their current standing would make sense only if the unit of analysis was the total situation, which includes the Pacaa Nova, the Brazilians, and the nature of their inter-relation. The acculturation approach tended to neglect or at least minimize some of the more important aspects of the overall situation: with its focus on the two subsystems and its emphasis on the interchange of cultural elements, it cannot account for many features of the contemporary predicament, such as exploitation, racism, and the effects that these have on the subordinate group. Acculturation studies have, in short, traditionally shied away from the realities of power and from the analysis of power relationships. The real picture of Sagarana would be obscured by treating the two cultures as subsystems, for they are inextricably linked and are part of one structure whose dynamics require analysis. As Roberto Cardoso de Oliveira points out, it is the nature of the power relationship and of conflict within the inter-ethnic system that must be explained. Since the Brazilians have the power, it is they who call the tune to which the Pacaa Nova must dance.

The process of change, initiated by sudden massive contact of a small-scale horticultural society by Western industrial society, has been described by Brazilian anthropologists as deculturation, or detribalization, rather than acculturation. Detribalization more adequately describes the dislocation and disorganization initiated by the impact of external forces that have characterized inter-ethnic contact in Brazil in this century. Once permanent contact is established, groups like the Pacaa Nova are quickly brought to economic, social, and psychological crisis; they are so hard hit that they rarely recover as functional social units.

Roberto Cardoso de Oliveira (1964) has suggested that Indian/Brazilian relations be seen as examples of internal colonialism — that settlements like Sagarana are better understood as products of a colonial relationship rather than as a culture. This concept was also used by Mexican anthropologists and sociologists to describe the situation of the native population of that country, and, following them, Colby and Van den Berghe (1969:3), define internal colonialism as a state where an independent country has within its own boundaries given special legal status to groups that differ culturally from the dominant group, and has created a distinct administrative machinery to handle such groups.

Often, this is brought about by actual conquest and subjugation. The administrative machinery may be part of the state, or be allocated to other institutions of the dominant society such as a religious group. In such cases, the state may maintain ultimate control, or may delegate such control.

There are a number of advantages of analyzing Sagarama as an instance of interal colonialism. First, it focuses attention on the nature of the total society within which inter-ethnic relations take place. Second, it directs attention to the outstanding feature of these inter-ethnic relations — the dominance of one group over another and the conflict between the two. Finally, a situation that seems to be a limited and purely aboriginal problem comes to be seen in the context of similar structural situations throughout the world, and can benefit from a much broader range of analysis and a comparative perspective.

As I looked at the history of the area and the evolution of its inter-ethnic relations, I realized that the pressures that led to contact and shaped social relations between Brazilians and the native population were predominantly economic. In the colonial period, the search for gold and slaves launched predatory bands of Portuguese and Spaniards along the river highways of the Amazon and its tributaries. The richest and most densely occupied environments along the main streams were virtually depopulated by a succession of diseases and slave traders. Those who escaped fled into the interior, displacing other ethnic groups along the way. In the late nineteenth and early twentieth century, rubber gatherers, responding to the incentive of spiralling prices, swarmed up the river systems to the south of the Great Stream in search of rubber ; along the way they established the socio-economic system that is still reflected in current social and political relations on the frontier.

The following study focuses on the historical factors and currents that led to the inter-ethnic situation at Sagarana, and offers an analysis of the nature of the social relations at the mission. It is not the study of a native community, since during the period of my research no strong sense of community had arisen, although there were some signs that the basis for such a community would emerge out of a common sense of oppression.

THE LAND

The Pacaa Nova inhabited the western part of the state of Rondônia. They ranged over a large area between the Serra dos Pacaas Novas and the Guaporé river valley, including the headwaters of the Mutum Paraná, Rio Riberão, Rio Lage, and the land drained by the Rios Pacaas Novas, Ouro Preto, and their tributaries.

In the east, the forest slopes upward toward the granite masses of the Serra de Pacaas Novas. Part of the Brazilian shield, this area has recently emerged as an important source of cassiterite or tin. In the west, it falls to the alluvial basins of the Madeira and Mamoré rivers, and in the south and west it melts into the seasonally flooded flat savanna plain known as the Llanos de Mojos. The area is crossed by numerous rivers and streams, which flood much of the forest during the rainy season and turn the lower reaches of the rivers into a great lake. The flooding becomes less pronounced as one moves upriver to higher country.

The climate is equatorial humid; on the average it rains 140 days per year with a total annual rainfall in the vicinity of about 2000 mm. There are two distinct seasons: a rainy season from September to April, during which it rains frequently but with variable intensity and duration, and a dry season from June to September, with little humidity and almost no precipitation. During the rains the interior is accessible by boat, although the upper reaches of the rivers are narrow.

It is in this latter zone that the Pacaa Nova were concentrated and where they were relatively safe from intruders, who would not risk an ambush on these narrow streams.

The dry season is quite severe. Water levels drop drastically, rendering even larger rivers like the Rio Pacaas Novas unnavigable during July and August. Although canoe travel halts during those months, foot travel is easy, and for the Pacaa Nova, who did not use canoes before contact, this is a time for visiting and ceremonial activity.

A dramatic feature of the dry season is the phenomenon of *friagem*, a cold spell caused by a wind from the south, which carries with it frigid air that drives the temperature down to as low as six or eight degrees centigrade for periods of up to one week. It is a raw and chilling cold, which is often accompanied by rain and may lead to the suspension of regular activities. The Pacaa Nova generally huddle around a fire or actually light fires under their hammocks or platform beds.

In general, there is little difference in temperature between the two seasons, but the intense sun of the dry season makes the heat of the day seem greater. Dry season nights are refreshing and, towards morning, even a little cool.

The land is densely forested and nurtures a great variety of plant species that provide the native and peasant population with most of their necessities. Of greatest importance are the palms: they are used for roofing, floors and walls of buildings, carrying baskets, bows, clubs, and also provide a variety of foods in the form of nuts and palm cabbage (palmito). Vines serve medicinal purposes and yield the poison *timbo* (*Derris sp.*) that is used for dry season fishing. Gums and resins of trees provide the raw materials for torches and the glue used to attach feathers to arrow shafts. Leaves, roots, and barks yield medicines as well as pigments. The Pacaa Nova rely heavily on fruits and nuts, primarily Brazil nuts, tucum (*Astrocaryum tucuma*), and babassu (*Orbignia speciosa*). A very significant wild crop for both *civilizados* and contacted Indians is *Hevea brasiliensis,* a species of rubber tree native to Brazil and common to the Madeira river and its tributaries. It is a source of high-quality rubber. Its abundance in the area launched the penetration of the vast interior wilderness that led to the construction of the famous Madeira/Mamoré Railroad and the subsequent emergence of towns and cities to service the expansion. Although rubber trees are plentiful, they are widely scattered, so that their commercial exploitation is time consuming, and hence expensive.

The fauna of the region is as varied as the flora, with a vast variety of insects, birds, fish, reptiles, and mammals. Honey constitutes an important and much-sought-after food product, and a major remedy for snake bite. The Indians distinguish at least ten different types of honey-producing bees. The Pacaa Nova eat a variety of grubs, most of which are found during the clearing of the forest in the dry season. Anthropologists have in the past underestimated the importance of insects as a source of food, and especially of protein, because insects are eaten in the forest, and their importance in the overall diet has escaped recording. But insects also make human life in the forest a difficult and at times painful experience. One has only to be bitten by a fire ant, or one of the host of other stinging or biting insects, to appreciate this. Mosquitos, bees and wasps are a constant irritant and can make clearing the forest quite unpleasant. Leaf-cutting ants (*Atta sp.),* wreak havoc on the shoots of young cultigens. Parasites, such as ticks, lice, fleas, and cockroaches invade the house and the body, and make life miserable. Insects crawl under the skin, into bodily orifices, or under finger-nails or toe-nails and cause infection. And finally, along the main rivers, anophile mosquitos bring malaria, a disease that emerges in new forms which resist the drugs produced to treat it.

Birds are plentiful, both in the forest and along the shores of the rivers. They are hunted for food or feathers that are used in the decoration of dress, weapons, and musical instruments. Among the species most frequently hunted are various types of partridge, pheasant, quail (inambu, jacu, mutum), as well as ducks and geese. Members of the parrot family are killed primarily for their feathers. Macaws and Amazon parrots are also common as pets in native villages where they are periodically plucked. Predator and scavenger birds are common, but only larger varieties of hawks are hunted for their feathers and down, which are used for ritual purposes and in the manufacture of arrows. Small songbirds abound in the woods, but neither they nor the ever-present herons and storks are hunted.

A Pacaa Nova shooting fish at Sagarana.

Fish are relatively plentiful in rivers away from centers of population. They were especially common in silt-carrying rivers like the Mamoré, but the increasing civilizado penetration and the advent of commercial fishing has depleted them rapidly. The most common species taken are tambaqui, traira, dourado *(Caracideos)*, pescada *(Cienideos)*, curimata *(Characidae)*, surubim *(Pimelodideos)*, and some pirarucu *(Arapaima gigas)*. Fish constitute an important part of the diet of both natives and Brazilians. In the recent past, turtles abounded in the Mamoré, but because of overexploitation they have become quite rare, despite protective legislation by both the Bolivian and Brazilian governments. Alligators have also been, and continue to be, decimated for their hides depite the fact that the sale of alligator hides is illegal in Brazil. The ban has merely driven up the price and increased the demand. Flouting the law carries few risks since it is almost impossible to police these vast frontier areas. Other reptiles, such as snakes and lizards, are plentiful, but are generally not hunted by humans.

Although the forest seems rich in fauna, and especially in mammalian species, game is not abundant. Areas are quickly hunted out. The largest animals hunted for food are the giant tapirs, which may weigh well over 200 kilos. Also important are pigs, both the peccary or caititi *(Tayassu tayassu)*, which travel singly and weigh 15-20 kilos, and the queixada *(Tayassu albirostris)*, which weigh as much as 25-35 kilos and are found in herds of up to several hundred. In 1969, over seventy of these pigs wandered into the settlement of Sagarana; fifty of them were shot or clubbed to death. Deer are regularily hunted, as are monkeys, especially howler and spider monkeys. Smaller rabbit-sized rodents such as the cutia *(Dasyprocta aguti)*, the racoon-like quati *(Nasua narica)* and various types of armadillos are most frequently found in clearings or in secondary forest. Along the streams and rivers, paca *(Coelogenis paca)* are the most popular prize because of the quantity and richness of their meat. The capivara *(Hydrochoerus sp.)*, the largest rodent in South America, roams the same shore, but is rarely taken for food because of its musty odour. In more recent times, carnivores, especially jaguars and other smaller jungle cats, have been hunted for their hides, which were marketed through Bolivia where legislation for their protection was less vigorous.

Removing hair of a monkey prior to roasting.

Native groups have long exploited the area through a combination of foraging, hunting, fishing, and slash and burn cultivation. Large numbers of outsiders first moved into the region around the latter part of the nineteenth century in search of rubber, but withdrew again when prices collapsed. Immigration picked up again in 1945 and has continued since that time. Despite this, the area's population density continues to be low.

Historical Background

The geographic region occupied by the Pacaa Nova was first visited by Europeans in the seventeenth century, as part of Iberian expansion from their original footholds in the New World. The Spaniards had moved down into the lowlands from the Andes and had encountered the Portuguese, who were pushing inland from the Atlantic coast. Between them, they had penetrated all of the major rivers, and their activities had wide-ranging effects throughout the Amazon drainage system. Their occupation of the major riverine environments had destroyed or displaced the populous tribal groups that inhabited these environments, and initiated a dynamic that touched even the remotest indigenous groups.

The invasion of what was later to be known as western Rondônia came from three centres of European occupation. The first came from Belém do Pará at the mouth of the Amazon and moved along the Amazon River into the Madeira. A second thrust came from the region of São Paulo and moved in a north-westerly direction into present day Mato Grosso and down the Guaporé River. The third descended from the Bolivian Andes to Santa Cruz de la Sierra, and from there headed into the grasslands of the Llanos de Mojos.

The Iberians' most dramatic impact on the region was without doubt the devastating effects of the diseases that they introduced, diseases that decimated the local Indian population and transformed the area into one of the most insalubrious on the continent.

The Madeira Frontier

In response to rumours of great wealth, the Portuguese from Belém moved up the Amazon and into the Madeira River. Reports of silver in the upper Madeira and indications of the presence of Spaniards in the area above the falls between present day Pôrto Velho and Guajará Mirim convinced the governor of Pará to send troops to explore the area and locate the Spanish. Some members of this expedition remained in the region and founded a settlement at Trocano, between the Jamari and the first rapids of the Madeira (Fonseca 1875:230).

But the Madeira region in the eighteenth century was primarily a zone of missionary activity — a missionary frontier. Jesuits first entered the area in 1669-72, partly in response to information that the enemies of Portugal, the Dutch, were trading with the Indians there. The missions they founded tended to be small in comparison to the Jesuit villages on the Amazon or in Mojos. For example, the population of San Antonio das Cachoeiras in 1730 was only 338 (Leite 1938-50, 111:15), compared to towns of three to five thousand in the latter areas.

The presence of different ethnic groups at each mission generated a great deal of friction, which often erupted into violence. As a result, there was constant movement in and out of the mission. The Indians were lured into the settlements by trade goods, or driven into them by fear of slave hunters, but were often unable to adjust to the strict regime of the missionaries. Some fled when the terrible epidemics came to the villages, and carried the new diseases, primarily measles, smallpox, and influenza, to their neighbours in the forest. The extent of the mortality caused by these diseases is impossible to reconstruct, but Fonseca (1975:227) reported that a single smallpox epidemic could easily eliminate thirty percent of a mission population. From the eighteenth century on, Indian communities were also plagued by malaria, a disease unknown prior to the conquest.

The region was also entered repeatedly by armed bands from Pará, in search of Indian slaves. Slaving expeditions continued throughout the eighteenth century, much to the chagrin of the missionaries, who were attempting to pacify the area and concentrate Indians in settlements along the main streams. The slavers did not hesitate to seize Indians on their way to the mission (Hugo 1959:1:34), or even to attack the mission posts themselves if they knew that the padres were absent (Leite 1938:111:329). The hostility generated by slaving activities forced mission posts to constantly relocate in order to escape destruction by Indian war parties seeking revenge. The Torá, a tribe linguistically related to the Pacaa Nova, were the most famous avengers, attacking Portuguese boats all the way up to the Rio Solimões. A punitive expedition sent by the governor of Pará finally crushed the Torá, enslaving some and driving the rest to the southeast into the Xingu river area. However, warfare continued unabated in the Madeira region. One hostile group succeeded another: Torá, Mura, Parintintin, and finally the Pacaa Nova.

Careful perusal of the literature indicates that, besides mission activity, there was some Portuguese settlement in the area in the eighteenth century. Fonseca (1875:235) talks about a cacao plantation at the mouth of the Aripuana, and Ricardo Franco (1857:265) mentions known locations of mines (presumably gold) at the Rio Riberão and Jamari.

Missionaries' accounts and official exploratory expeditions indicate that the Portuguese exploited the area's natural resources. Ricardo Franco (1857:253-254) reports that hundreds of boats from Pará annually congregated at the beaches near Santo Antonio to collect turtle eggs for the production of oil. Many boats gathered on the Madeira, especially near the mouth of the Jamari, to harvest the great abundance of high quality wild cacao (Fonseca 1875:249). Consistent with the usual Portuguese practice, the crews of these expeditions initiated relations with Indian groups in order to obtain supplies (Davidson 1970:9). However, the Madeira region remained insecure and unpacified.

Despite movement along the Madeira itself, most of the vast hinterland remained unexplored territory. The few Portuguese in the area clustered around the main river, engaged essentially in subsistence and supplementing their income through extractive activity or by provisioning passing boats.

The Guaporé Frontier

The second major thrust that ultimately led to the occupation of the Guaporé and Mamoré river system came from São Paulo. The search for gold and slaves brought large numbers of Portuguese, mestizo and mulatto *bandeirantes* (bands of explorers and adventurers) far into the interior of the Mato Grosso, and initiated a rivalry between the established Spaniards in the west and the Portuguese, who were advancing from the east.

The discovery of gold near present-day Cuiabá by the expedition of Antonio Pires de Campos (Roquette Pinto 1954:a) was the beginning of a burst of territorial expansion that by 1734 reached the Guaporé River. In the 1730s, prospectors moved into the Serra de São Vicente and established mining camps. The small settlements of prospectors needed food and a cheap labour force. Indians were either driven off and robbed of the produce from their gardens, or they were enslaved and forced to dig and pan the soil of the gold camps. The Portuguese Crown encouraged settlement of the area and began to build trading and military posts (Fonseca 1875:290-91). The economy was entirely dependent on gold, for only that precious metal could justify the extensive capital outlay required to occupy and administer such a remote region (Davidson 1970:110).

By 1742, Manoel Felix da Lima, a prospector, had established the feasibility of a direct link with the Portuguese colony of Pará, via the

Guaporé, Mamoré, Madeira and Amazonas rivers. The Portuguese found it especially crucial to secure this vital route, since the only alternative was an overland journey of six months to São Paulo.

In the early 1740s, the yield of gold near Vila Bela had declined drastically. Prospectors moved north on the Guaporé in search of new sources. One of these groups was made up of Portuguese fugitives who settled on the Guaporé at Ilha Comprida. They raided Indian villages (including nearby Spanish Jesuit villages) for slaves, and generally robbed and cheated the native population, but were tolerated by the Crown because they helped secure the border against the Spaniards. Fonseca (1875:335) notes: "The truth is that but for those lawless men who dwell there, the Spaniards would have advanced further upstream."

In view of the discovery of gold and the constant Spanish threat, the Portuguese Crown officially designated the area as the Captaincy of Mato Grosso in 1748. A year later, an expedition was dispatched from Pará to Mato Grosso to survey the area and report in detail on the location, extent, and strength of the Spanish missions. Neither side really knew much about the other. One member of that expedition, José Gonçalves da Fonseca, in his diary left the first detailed description of the Madeira, Mamoré, and Guaporé river valleys. Fonseca notes the desire of both Spaniards and Portuguese to win over the indigenous population as allies in the conflict over the area, and points out that at that early date, iron already played an important role in bringing Indians into contact:

"Ameoes, Guaiorotes have permitted traffic with the Portuguese more readily than with the Spanish priests who began catechising them without making them presents of cutlery which they especially value." (1875:333-334).

Constant confrontation and strategic manoeuvres, as well as military and diplomatic activity, marked the period 1750-70. The border issue was finally settled by the 1750 Treaty of Madrid, and two Spanish Jesuit missions on the east side of the Guaporé were forced back to the west. In 1752, the Portuguese established their own mission a few miles north of the Corumbiara River, among bands of Mequen and Guajarata.

Domesticated Indians within the Portuguese missions were strictly disciplined and were exploited for their labour in a system reminiscent of the forced labour service *repartimiento* of the Spanish colonial areas. The missions were obliged to provide rowers (*Serviço Real*) to any government expedition in the area. Both Fonseca (1749) and Ricardo

Franco (1785) used this service, and refer to the reluctance of the Indians to leave the security of their tribal territory, since most of them never came back. Sickness was obviously so common that Ricardo Franco (1857:262) was led to suggest the establishment of a post in the area of the falls where sick Indians could be exchanged for healthy ones.

Indians were also used in construction, and in the mines as slaves. However, free Indian labour was not very effective in the tropical forest, where no state structures existed and leaders did not have the authority to order their followers about. Only very strict supervision prevented those dissatisfied with conditions from returning to the surrounding forest. As in much of the New World, Indian labour had to be replaced by black slaves who were less likely to flee into an unknown forest and were more easily recaptured.

Black slaves brought from Sãe Paulo were used both in the mines and to grow crops to feed miners. Some of them did manage to escape, fleeing into the forest and, together with friendly Indians or captured Indian women, formed small settlements called *quilombos.* Ricardo Franco witnessed the destruction of several such mixed settlements by Portuguese expeditions from Vila Bella (1857:236).

The expulsion of the Jesuits from Portuguese territory in 1759 spelled the end of Catholic mission activity in the area. Most Indians filtered back into the forest, not to be contacted again until the late nineteenth or twentieth century.

Spanish Occupation Of The Mojos Plains

The pursuit of gold and silver brought the Spaniards into the lowland areas of eastern Bolivia, where rumour and myth spoke of an El Dorado-like figure known as the Great Paititi. In the early seventeenth century, several expeditions entered the Mojos plains via present-day Santa Cruz de la Sierra, but found no gold. The region was finally brought into the Spanish orbit by the Jesuits, who entered it after 1668. Jesuits carried on missionary work in the Mojos and the neighbouring Chiquitos province for one hundred years, until they were expelled in 1767. During that period, they founded twenty-one missions. One or two priests ran each mission under a political—economic system that Denevan calls socialistic, and that was similar to the famous "Mission Republics" of the Jesuits in Paraguay.

For the tribes in the Mojos plain, missionization was a decisive event. The organization of Indians into central mission settlements meant the destruction of traditional political and social st... well as total socio-economic reorganization and incorpo... Spanish colonial society through a system of peasant towns v... ly Spanish organization. Although the Jesuits taught in the r... guage and incorporated some Indian cultural details, the eco... social activities were strictly organized and centered around the cycle of Catholic religious feasts.

From the beginning, the Mojos and Chiquitos missions played a critical role in the border conflict. In 1724, after a number of Portuguese reconnaissance parties had been sent down the Madeira from Pará and incursion by slavers had become more frequent, the viceroy of Peru ordered the Indians to be armed and instructed in the arts of war (Davidson 1973:97).

Along the shores of the Guaporé and Mamoré, both the Spaniards and the Portuguese attempted to use the mission Indians as pawns in their struggle over control of the interior. However, the tropical forest Indians there were not amenable to resettlement and mission control; they were traditionally organized in small independent settlements and did not thrive in the nucleated mission posts.

The major impact of Spanish penetration on the native population was demographic. As in the Portuguese missions, diseases decimated the Indians. Denevan (1966), who documented the severe decline, estimates that the population dropped from a minimum of 100,000 in 1690 to 30–35,000 in 1737. Padre Zapata, writing in 1695, reports continuous sickness, smallpox, tuberculosis, malaria, and dysentery among the tribes of the lower Guaporé.

After the Jesuit expulsion and the disintegration of the Spanish missions on the east bank of the Guaporé, most small tribal groups returned to the forest and were lost to permanent contact. The exact degree to which they were affected by the missions is difficult to determine in the absence of earlier information on Indian groups in the area, as well as subsequent lack of contact. Among most groups, little of the Jesuit teaching seems to have remained, a fact that led Heath (1966:148) to refer to it as perhaps one of the most abrupt instances of "deculturation" in world history. Fonseca (1880:190) notes that some of the groups he contacted still used some words of obvious Spanish derivation, but no longer remembered where they came from. Nordenskiold (1924:252) was told by rubber tappers that at the end of August the Huaynam celebrated a feast with maize beer and dancing that might be a remnant of the mission period, since the feast of Santa Rosa falls on August 30.

The Moré retained little of their mission past; they became a major threat to occupation of the area at the confluence of the Guaporé-Mamoré in the latter part of the nineteenth and early part of the twentieth century.

The impact of the expulsion was much greater in the Mojos and Chiquitos areas, where the missionaries were firmly in control and enjoyed great prestige. Although secular clergy took the place of the Jesuits, the communities suffered a great population and cultural decline. Denevan (1966:33) points out that the fifteen major mission towns in the Mojos with a population in excess of 30,000 were reduced to eleven towns with a population of less than 20,000 in the years between 1767 and 1788.

The Rubber Era

In the nineteenth century, the demands of rapid industrialization in Europe opened up new export possibilities for the young republics of Latin America. Economic opportunities created by price fluctuations on the commodity markets of New York, Frankfurt and Paris gave shape to the cycles of expansion and contraction and directly translated themselves into pressure on the lands of small indigenous tribal and band societies in the depth of the forest. The great surge in demand and the sky-rocketing prices of rubber at the turn of the century determined the extinction or absorption of innumerable tribal groups, especially in the rubber-rich areas to the south of the Amazon.

Rubber is made from the dried latex of a number of species of trees, but predominantly *Hevea brasiliensis*, which yields the best and most copious latex and which, in the nineteenth century, grew exclusively in Amazonia. Although it had been described by early travellers, its commercial development had to await Charles Goodyear's process of vulcanization in 1839.

By 1858, over 10,000 workers in the United States alone were involved in the making of rubber goods. However, production was still comparatively low. It was Dunlop's patent to produce tires that in the 1880s provided the great stimulus to mass production. Within a short time, rubber became Brazil's number three export, after coffee and sugar. Demand and prices continued to spiral upwards in the first part of the twentieth century.

The search for rubber sent waves of men up major rivers and along most tributaries. The main movement emanated from Pará and pushed up the Amazon. Whereas in the latter part of the nineteenth century the most important centre had been Belém, the focus in the early twentieth century shifted to Manáus, which soon grew into a major commercial centre with a population in excess of fifty thousand. Vast fortunes were made, and major American and European commercial houses established branches there. With its wealth and flourishing cultural life, Manáus came to be referred to as the Paris of the Amazon. It boasted all the modern facilities of the times, including a palatial opera house which was built at a cost of over two million uninflated dollars (Gauld 1964:108/Burns 1965).

Brazilian Amazonia grew rapidly in population, from approximately 149,000 in 1832, to 386,370 in 1890, and 1,346,673 in 1920 (Reis 1953:36). The first migrants from the impoverished northeast, the *Nordestinos*, entered the area in the 1860s, but the real influx came in the late 1870s and 1880s, following a series of severe droughts and famines in that area. In 1878, over fifteen thousand entered Amazonia from the state of Ceará alone. Although most of the migration into Amazonia came via Belém and Manáus, there were other movements of population from the west and south, from Bolivia, Peru, and Mato Grosso, where rubber production almost doubled yearly in the late 1880s (Fifer 1966:363). In the early period, expansion was especially rapid, and trees were drained of their total supply so that the movement was actually nomadic, with rubber men moving on to new supplies (Reis 1953:64). In twenty to thirty years, virtually all of the vast region of the Amazon had been explored, especially the richer rubber districts of the south bank tributaries of the "Great Stream."

The Madeira region became a major centre for the production of this new commodity and began to be coveted for its "black gold" by both Bolivia and Brazil. Established agriculture and extraction of other products were suspended as workers all switched to rubber. Men became crazed by the prospect of rubber, selling their ranches and cattle to go into the business (Health 1882:134). Bolivians were the first to be involved in the extraction of rubber in the Madeira region. Most of them came from the "Oriente" of Bolivia and brought with them a work force of Mojo, Mobima and Cayubaba Indians, the remnants of the former populous Jesuit towns. (Keller 1874/Pinkas 1887:294). By 1899, 60,000 Brazilians were already in the Acre area, which was claimed but not controlled by Bolivia. An independence movement by the Brazilian rubber tappers and the resultant confrontation and outbreak of fighting between Bolivia and Brazil led to the Treaty of Petropolis and the ceding of the rubber-rich territory of Acre to Brazil in 1903.

The Rubber Extractive Frontier

Rubber extraction created a social system that reflected the nature of its economic structure. At the base of the system were the rubber tappers and the various labourers, who located the trees and cut the trails. They were employed by the "owners" of rubber concessions, the *seringalistas*. Self-made men who had paid a fee to the government in return for the rights to exploit a given territory, the seringalistas opened up the trails, recruited the rubber tappers, provided tools, and supplied food for the first season. Since a substantial amount of credit was required for the operation of a sizeable seringal or estate, they became dependent on the large credit and commercial houses which operated in Manáus.

The scope of rubber operations varied as prices rose, but tended to grow in size toward the end of the nineteenth century. In the Beni and Madeira areas, large concerns became more dominant; small operators were often squeezed out by their creditors, with owners becoming managers (Pinkas 1887:294). In eastern Bolivia in particular, very large enterprises such as Suarez, Vaca Diez, Vazques, and Braillard were the rule. In 1909, Vaca Diez had registered 4,278 rubber trails, and Suarez 20,758. Immense credit and great speculation characterized these endeavours.

The average seringal cut a narrow band on both sides of a river, often for fifty to seventy miles. Normally, it did not extend more than two or three miles into the interior. The *seringueros* (rubber tappers) were either scattered in isolated family groups throughout the area, or lived in a central barrack-like residence *(barracão)*. The latter arrangement was more common during the "rush" itself, since many of the employees were single men, whereas the scattered model is more prevalent today. In both cases, the seringal consisted of a large structure, barracão, which provided facilities for storage; the office; perhaps the home of the seringalista or his manager; and in all cases, a store, usually within a day's travel of even the remotest sections. The term "seringal" is used to refer to the physical structure as well as the system of social and economic relations. Between seringalista and seringueiro no cash changed hands. In the contract drawn up between the two parties, employees were supplied with food (manioc flour, sugar, rice, beans, tinned meat and fish), kerosene, clothing, medicine, tools, and occasionally women, all on credit. In return, they were obliged to deliver the whole harvest to the seringalista. The seringalista usually paid prices for rubber well below the market value: up to 40 to 50 percent below, and charged prices well above the market value of the supplies. Consequently, the seringueiros was always in debt; they were obliged to make purchases at the company store but were rarely able to pay their bills in full. The rubber tappers were frequently cheated, starting life in the seringal deeply in debt for their transportation and tools. They were initially given poor rubber avenues so that expenses surpassed income, and became ever more closely tied to the barracão. Mostly illiterate, they were at the mercy of the *patrão* (boss) and his employees.

Rubber estate managers changed frequently. Many were adventurers and drifters, and since they were paid according to production, they drove their men very hard. Because of the remoteness of most seringais (plural of seringal) and the absence of other authority, the seringalista or his manager exercised great power and frequently enforced his law by means of gun or whip (Craig 1907:251). Seringalistas controlled the river entrances and exits to their territory and few tappers were able to escape their obligations.

The unsanitary conditions of most rubber camps bred widespread sickness and death. Especially serious were malaria, beriberi and intestinal problems. Lange (1911:34) reports that in a survey of 87 rubber tappers, sickness accounted for the loss of two work days per week on the average. Their diet, lacking in fresh fruit and vegetables, lowered their resistance to infection. At the same time they were discouraged or forbidden to grow their own food, or to spend valuable time fishing or hunting, in order that full time could be devoted to the cash crop. Although many of the rivers teemed with fish, the rubber tappers' diet was more likely to consist of tinned sardines.

The literature dealing with the rubber boom differentiated between two types of rubber tappers: the "Amazonense" or "Mato Grossense" and the "Nordestino". The former, adapted to life in the Amazon, was usually half Indian and lived on the seringal with his family. He frequently married Indian women, and incorporated aspects of Indian culture into his life in the forest. Most Nordestinos, on the other hand, were single or had left their families at home. Because they feared and were suspicious of Indians, they rarely married Indian women. The rubber camps, especially those consisting of Nordestinos, lacked women, and the few who were brought in were greatly desired and fought over. To ease the situation, the authorities occasionally emptied houses of prostitution in the cities and shipped the women off to the seringais (Reis 1953:123). These characteristics, and especially the lack of a normal family and community life, led Caspar (1957:289) to refer to the society of the seringal as a "part society," which presented the Indian population with whom it had contact with only a very limited, distorted view of Brazilian society: the dominantly male camps were characterized by large-scale drunkenness and violence. Nevertheless it was the Nordestino, once he had adjusted to the forest, who became the most efficient rubber tapper and cut the most rubber.

To maintain order and production, the seringalistas often acted arbitrarily and, given the isolation of the barracão, could usually do so with impunity. The conditions favoured violent men who could maintain sufficient order to gather their harvest.

Rubber and the Indian

More than any other event, or series of events, the steady advance of rubber gatherers and their extensive use of land spelled the doom of the native population. The opening up of vast new areas to economic exploitation brought large numbers of Indians into contact with Brazilians. To a much greater degree than during the colonial period, epidemics of measles, smallpox, and influenza devastated the native population. Most of the tribes of the Beni forest, the Madeira and Mato Grosso disappeared in the wake of invasion by rubber tappers. Within fifty to sixty years, over seventy percent of the tribes of present-day Rondônia had become extinct, and many others had dwindled to groups of only a few dozen or so. Most of the Chapacuran-speaking tribes in the forest area, the Jarú, the Urupá, the Pawumwa (Huanyam), all close linguistic relatives of the Pacaa Nova, disappeared.

The rubber frontier, because its product demanded a greatly dispersed settlement pattern, was spread over a vast area. Unlike the situation during the colonial period, when the Portuguese restricted themselves to the main rivers, rubber tappers were now scattered throughout the interior, vying with Indians for limited natural resources.

Because the Nordestinos were unfamiliar with Indians and consequently feared them, the first encounters between the two peoples were usually hostile. Rubber tappers from the northeast usually shot at the first sight of "wild" Indians (Pinkas 1887:298). In short, the rubber extractive frontier was characterized by intermittent, hostile contact, which often made a particular area unsafe for the rubber interests.

Therefore, Indians had to be either driven out or integrated into the rubber-gathering economy.

In Rondônia, the frontier encroached into the territory of small bands of Indians who were attempting to evade the intruders. The Pacaa Nova were quite successful in avoiding these encounters.

"Tame" Indians were frequently used as guides, rowers or hunters, or performed general camp duties rather than put to work as rubber tappers. They were also used to lure others to the camps. One of the most effective inducements to establish such contacts were iron tools. Not infrequently, "wild" tribes such as the Moré and Acanga Pirangas raided white settlements for these tools, or stole them while the owners slept (Pinkas 1887:299). Herndon and Gibbon, in 1854, noted that uncontacted Caripuna already possessed trade knives and fishhooks as well as domesticated chickens, and initiated contact with passing travellers to obtain replacements.

At the barracão, the Indians were exposed to a segment of white society made up of drifters, many without families, who had little regard for law and who were often drunk and violent. In some cases, the "tame" Indians served to mediate the first contact, and the barracão thus served as an intermediate place in the transition from Indian to civilizado. Caspar (1957:289-290) writes, "There is no doubt that the Barracão Indians served for the Tuparí as a type of achievable model. As people who participated in both worlds, they cushioned the shock that the contact with rubber gatherers on their trips to São Luis was bound to have on the Tuparí." Few tribal groups survived the disintegrating effects of sustained contact with the barracão; removed from their society, they entered the new one at the bottom of the social scale.

The Madeira-Mamoré Railway

Brazilian expansion along the Madeira River from the north, the Bolivian thrust in the Beni, and the development of the seringais on the Mamoré and its rubber-rich tributaries, were blocked by the formidable obstacle of falls stretching for over 200 miles between present-day Pôrto Velho and Guajará Mirim. The falls effectively cut off three thousand miles of navigable tributaries and rich rubber lands from the main stream and from access to the markets of Manáus. This obstacle was already a major concern in the eighteenth century because it provided a barrier to the movement of goods and men between Mato Grosso and Pará.

Transportation past the falls was both dangerous and expensive. The trip upriver took nine weeks; downriver, three weeks. The area was notorious for disease, especially yellow fever. In a bad year, deaths among crews were as high as fifty percent. Pearson (1911:121) reports that approximately fifteen percent of the rubber was lost at the falls, and transportation costs averaged between eight hundred to twelve hundred dollars per ton of cargo.

As early as 1867, two German engineers, Joseph and Franz Keller, were commissioned by the Brazilian government to survey the Madeira falls and examine the feasibility of a railway, road, or canal around them. Although the Kellers spent several months in the area, they say little about the aboriginal population.

Through the latter part of the nineteenth century, several attempts were made to build a railroad around the falls. By 1873 one company had surveyed 320 miles of jungle and cleared a hundred-foot swath for twenty-five miles; its workers had laid a track for one-quarter of a mile and were operating a locomotive on it before the project was finally abandoned. The company that was to complete the project began work on the railroad in August 1907. The stretch linking Pôrto Velho and Guajará Mirim was completed in July 1912. More than twenty-five thousand workmen from Greece, Italy, England, Germany, Portugal, the West Indies, Central Europe, and northeastern Brazil were employed over the five-year period. Over six thousand men died during the construction, including three American doctors (Ferreira 1961; Gauld 1964:313).

Relations with the Indians were at this point infrequent and mostly peaceful. Pearson (1911:128) claims that they supplied the work camps with turtle and fish. The company strictly regulated contact with these aboriginal groups. Percival Farquhar, a Quaker and the president of the company, demanded that all of the men sign a contract wherein they agreed to pay no court to the Caripuna women nor to sell firearms to the men (Amm Folder 1036, 1913 Hugo 1959:11:339). The general manager of the company even suggested bonuses for rubber tappers who succeeded in making peaceful contacts with Indian groups in the area. Despite this, some hostilities did occur, and Indians as well as some workers were killed. Six German workers on their way downriver were slain in 1908 and their heads displayed on poles by the river bank (Gauld 1964:127). Reprisals were discouraged by the company.

The construction of the railroad brought other economic activity into the area. It resulted in the establishment of settlements at the two terminals (which later grew into Pôrto Velho and Guajará Mirim), the two major cities in Rondônia, and encouraged the growth of commercial agriculture along the route, especially the production of fruits and vegetables to feed the work teams. But after the termination of the railway contract and a decline in rubber production, these small sites along the river were slowly abandoned. The promise of cheap transportation led to the establishment of seringais by larger entrepreneurs, including some foreign firms. The railway company itself was granted the vast region from the Mutum Paraná to Guajará Mirim and inland to the Serra dos Parecís, approximately one million hectares (Ashmead 1911:449). The company was also granted six million acres in Bolivia by General Ismael Montes, the president of that country.

Throughout its planning and construction, the railway had encouraged exploration and mapping of the region. One of the reconnaissance expeditions, led by Thorwald Loch, a Danish engineer, ascended the Rio Pacaas Novas in 1904, accompanied by sixteen Bolivians in four boats. Loch studied a total of seventy-three kilometers of river, which would have put him into the area inhabited by the Pacaa Nova in 1960. However, he reported nothing of the native population.

At the time of its inception, the railroad promised a great future for the interior of South America, not just for its rubber, but also for its agriculture and cattle. Contemporary writers were often ecstatic about its potential:

"This seemingly obscure railway in the jungle will ultimately carry on its road-bed more traffic and do more to develop an area almost boundless in extent and potential ties than the 10,000 miles of Cape to Cairo and Pan American together (Bull. of Pan American Union 1910:30-32)."

Sixty years later, the same was claimed for the highway that crosses the vastness of the Amazonian jungle. But, like the railroad, doubts of its viability are already being raised, and the initial optimism is being replaced by a more realistic appraisal of Amazon development.

The Decline of Rubber

In 1911, after rubber had reached the glorious but artificially high price of over three dollars per pound, the bubble burst. For the first time, rubber production on plantations in the Orient exceeded Brazilian production. Prices plummeted from $2.06 per pound in 1910 to .82 cents in 1913. This sudden dip brought on the collapse of a number of credit houses that were hopelessly over-extended, as well as the insolvency of many smaller producers. Under the existing structure, rubber tappers could no longer earn enough to cover expenses no matter how hard they worked. The new Madeira-Mamoré railway, which was to be the key to the wealth of the region, had started with three trains per week in 1912, but by 1913 had dropped to one per week for lack of cargo. In that year, Brazil still produced forty percent of the world's rubber, but that percentage decreased to six percent by 1920, and the price dropped to .35 cents per pound. Brazil was simply unable to compete with plantation rubber. In the Amazon, costs of production were more than double those of Malaya and Ceylon.

The collapse of rubber prices dealt a shattering blow to an economy totally built around, and dependent on, that product. Financial houses, their foundation pulled out from under them, went bankrupt and great fortunes were lost. Opulent urban centres like Manáus reverted to somnolent fishing and peasant villages; the strong foreign presence and foreign capital vanished overnight; seringais were deserted and the rural population declined.

Rubber tappers with the capital to do so left the region, especially the more recent arrivals from the Nordeste. Others supplemented subsistence activities with hauling wood as fuel for the steamers and the railway. Agricultural concerns on the Guaporé diversified. Besides rubber and brazil nuts, tappers began to grow coffee and sugar-cane for the local market.

The decline of rubber relieved the pressure on the remaining uncontacted Indian groups. The Pacaa Nova would most likely have been contacted forty years sooner if expansion had continued at the same pace. Throughout the 1920s and 1930s, prices continued to drop and the rubber avenues became vacant as more Nordestinos packed up and returned home. The exodus reached its climax circa 1932 when rubber prices reached an all-time low. This depopulation resulted in chronic labour shortages when demand for rubber for the local market rose again during the late 1930s and later in the 1950s and 1960s.

Japanese ambition and the outbreak of the Second World War gave the Brazilian rubber industry renewed vitality. The U.S. once again looked to Brazil for its rubber and the seringais experienced a surge in activity, although not a rise in price (in fact, the price of rubber was frozen over the war years).

A joint U.S.-Brazilian campaign referred to as the "Batalha de Borracha" (Rubber Battle) was organized to revitalize the seringais of the

Amazon region. It was financed by five million dollars and brought an influx of U.S. personnel and technology into the area. Its immediate aim was to push production to 70,000 tons, an objective that was never to be reached for lack of labour and infrastructure. Large numbers of Nordestinos, 24,300 according to Reis (1953:76), were transported back into Amazonia between 1942 and 1945. Caspar (1957:287) claims that the jails of Manáus were emptied and the inmates shipped to the abandoned seringais of the Madeira. Most of the Syrians and Lebanese, or "Turcos," who were to dominate the rubber trade and retail enterprises in Guajará Mirim, came at the beginning of the war years. At the end of the war, in 1945, the avenues were not deserted but continued to expand at a moderate rate.

During the late 1930s and the 1940s, tribes in the interior of the Madeira and Guaporé were again brought into contact with rubber tappers, or were contacted by the agricultural enterprises along the Guaporé (Snethlage 1937). The Makuráp, Jabotí, Guajuru, Aruá, Purubora, Moré, and later, the Tuparí, were brought into the orbit of the extractive system at this time. Rubber tappers started to move up the Rio Pacaas Novas and neighbouring rivers in greater numbers, and by the 1950s development had reached the headwaters. Guerra (1953:221) claims there were 789 rubber tappers on the Rio Pacaas Novas alone. Hostile encounters with Indians near the Rio Madeira, Bananeiras, Riberão, Pacaas Novas, and Ouro Preto continued over many years, at great cost in lives to both sides.

The economy of the whole territory depended on rubber. In 1950, 6,567 men worked in rubber as opposed to 2,632 in agriculture, and Rondônia was Brazil's number three producer. Increasing hostilities impeded the exploitation of rubber; it threatened the lives of rubber tappers and their families, as well as the profits of the owners of the seringais. With the rise in prices, the stakes became ever higher.

Indian unrest also threatened the work crews along the length of the Madeira-Mamoré railroad and appeared to endanger the city itself. The businessmen who dominated the local economy were only too happy to fuel rumours of Indians hiding in the very outskirts of the city. They manipulated and exaggerated rumours and aggravated existing fears and tensions in order to put greater pressure on the authorities to resolve the Indian threat once and for all. Although seringalistas and commercial interests controlled the expansion into Indian territory and ordered the launching of "punitive expeditions," the brunt of Indian defensive reaction was borne by the man in the field. The rubber tapper, vulnerable in his isolation, feared the Indian greatly. Newcomers from the northeast had heard tales of the grisly encounters between rubber men and the fiercely "cannibalistic" Pacaa Nova, whose knowledge of the forest made them a formidable foe. Over the years their resistence had become almost legendary. Rubber tappers took no chances — any naked brown figure was an instant target for a shotgun blast.

Motivated largely by revenge, the Indians took their deadly toll. These encounters led to an endless cycle of attacks and counter-attacks. The story of Adolfo is one of many, but it illustrates well the bitter and unmerciful conflict between civilizado and Indian. The account is unique in that we have both sides of the incident; that of the Oro nao Manim, who related his version to Richard Sollis of the New Tribes Missions, as well as that of Adolfo, whose tragedy was well known in the area. The version herein is essentially that of Manim. He had lost a brother to the bullets of a civilzado punitive expedition, and he was determined to avenge his brother's death. With several of his kinsmen, he set out for the great river, the Mamoré. On arrival at the mouth of the Rio Pacaas Novas, they remained hidden in a grove of trees, for there were many *wijam*, (civilizados) in this area. Within a short time they spotted a canoe heading directly for the beach below them. The dugout, carrying two men and two women, landed very close to their hiding place, and while one man remained behind to pull the boat up on the sandy beach, the three others started up the bank toward the forest where Manim and his men lay in wait. When they were quite close, the Indians let fly their arrows, wounding all three. The civilizados, in panic, fled down the beach. The third man ran along the shore to hide under the brush. As they fled, the younger of the two women, greatly hampered by her wound, began to fall back. With this opportunity at hand, Manim rushed forward, and grabbing her by the hair began to pull her back to the shelter of the forest. The wounded man, seeing her predicament, turned to help; he seized the woman's leg and for several minutes the two tugged at the screaming woman. The civilizado, a somewhat more robust man, managed to pull her closer to the canoe. As they approached the canoe, Manim spied a machette in the bow of the craft. Still maintaining his grip on his victim's hair, he swung around to the dugout, gripped the weapon, decapitated the struggling woman, and swiftly retreated to the security of the forest. Manim's opponent was Adolfo, and the woman, his wife. From that time on Adolfo became one of the Pacaa Nova's deadliest foes, lending his services to those who sought to rid the territory of Indians.

Even without the threat of attacks by "wild" Indians, the life of the isolated rubber tapper was an extremely difficult one. The widely distributed rural population rarely saw a doctor or a priest. Illnesses were common and were dreaded; if medical help was required it often took a week or more to get to the towns by canoe. Less serious cases meant loss of a work day, and income.

Despite the absence of most of the excesses of the boom period, life for the migrants from the northeast had changed little. They still tended to leave their wives and children at home, and ventured out as single men. Alone in the seringal, without a woman, they found the isolation unbearable and survival difficult. They entered into temporary liaisons and were rarely able to save adequate funds to send for their families. Seringalistas saw to it that they were kept dependent through debt.

I spent a week with Raimundo, a slight, ferret-faced, hungry-looking man who was cutting rubber on the Rio Pacaas Novas just below the Rio Negro. Like most of the rubber workers in the area, he was a Nordestino. He had been in Rondônia for fifteen years; at the time, he was working for one of the "Turco" seringalistas in Guajará Mirim, renting a house site and a rubber avenue for the equivalent of approximately $100 per year. The location was remote, nearly a half day's distance by canoe from his nearest neighbour. His small clearing by the side of the river contained several thatched huts standing in the shade of some large mango trees. Behind them, in the direction of the forest, a garden was planted with manioc, beans, sweet potatoes, and a few bananas. A three-by-four meter thatched hut with paxiuba sides served as living quarters. A small kitchen was attached to the back and a roofed extension provided storage on the side. About ten meters away stood an A-frame structure covered with palm fronds, used for curing the latex. Raimundo, a widower, lived with his three children, who performed most of the chores around the house while he made his daily rounds of the rubber avenues.

Raimundo invited me to accompany him one particular morning. The day began at around 4 a.m. while it was still dark. After a pungently sweet Brazilian coffee, we were ready to leave. It was best to start at the crack of dawn because the sap runs better in the early morning. Raimundo wore home-made rubber shoes, a ragged cotton shirt, and patched cotton trousers. On his head, strapped to his cap, was a small kerosene lamp. His gear consisted of a special curved knife, several hundred nested tin cups, and a shotgun with its handle cut to a pistol grip. We started off along a trail at the back of the house and within minutes had plunged into the forest. Walking at a brisk pace, we reached the first tree in fifteen minutes. It was a large old rubber tree *(hevea brasiliensis)*, already deeply scarred along five feet of its trunk. Raimundo pulled out a crudely made ladder from the bushes, climbed up beyond the scars, and made a fresh cut. He pushed a sharp-lipped metal cup into the bark below it and we continued on, winding our way through the forest, stopping periodically to repeat the procedure. Several times he stopped abruptly, unshouldered his gun, and listened, but that day he did not bring down any game to add variety to the monotonous diet of manioc and beans.

By 10 a.m. we were back at the clearing for some fish stew, manioc-flour, and a coffee. Despite the fact that Raimundo was short of both sugar and coffee, he felt obliged to show hospitality to a guest by offering the best he had. After a short rest, we set off again to retrace our steps. The tin cups were emptied into a three-gallon bucket that resembled an old-fashioned milk pail. By 1 p.m. we were back at the house.

Collecting the latex is only the first part of a rubber tapper's work. In the afternoon, Raimundo disappeared into the smokehouse, and within minutes, billows of whitish-grey smoke poured through the thatch. Inside the lean-to, the smoke from the excavated firepit was funnelled through a conical hood with a small opening at the top. A rack straddled the opening and held a round sapling that passed through a large oval ball of rubber. On one side of the opening stood a large aluminum dish. Raimundo sat in front of this structure, pulled up the large pan, and started to roll the sapling so that the large rubber ball began to rotate across the smoke; as it turned, he poured the milky liquid over it in such a way that the excess dripped into the aluminum pan. In this way, the ball of rubber grew until it weighed seventy-five to one hundred kilos, at which point a new one was started. The procedure, performed in a smoky hut during the heat of the dry season, is a chore that most rubber tappers dislike. The smoke irritates the eyes, and it is not uncommon for the older workers to go partially blind.

By 4 or 5 in the afternoon the latex had coagulated, and Raimundo turned his attention to fishing for the evening meal. It was after dark when the family finally sat down to a simple dinner of fish, manioc-flour and beans. The daily round was repeated six days a week during the dry season. Raimundo and his family spent Sundays visiting neighbours or just listening to the transistor radio purchased from the proceeds of the last harvest. From his labour he produced approximately 1,000 kg of rubber per season. The harvest depended on the richness of the seringal, but was also heavily influenced by Raimundo's health. It was not unusual to lose one-third of a season because of recurring bouts of malaria. Raimundo had vacillated between dependence on a seringalista, or semi-independence by renting his own rubber avenues. He said both systems had their advantages, in the first case, he would receive a cash advance; in the latter, he could take advantage of the competition between rubber buyers. He thought that in the future he might again work for one patron despite the lower returns for his production.

Raimundo cutting rubber on the Rio Pacaas Novas.

Smoking the latex.

No matter how rich the rubber avenue or how high the price, it was absolutely essential for rubber tappers to produce their own food — to maintain a garden, keep a few chickens, ducks, and perhaps a pig, and to hunt and fish for much of their protein. The cash earned through rubber provided other necessities: tools, medical treatment and drugs, clothing, kerosene, shotgun shells, batteries, fishing gear, coffee, sugar, powdered milk and rice, and a few luxuries such as a radio and one or two articles of clothing.

The rubber tappers along the Rio Pacaas Novas and its tributaries were a mixed group. Many were from the Brazilian northeast, others came from Mato Grosso or Amazonas. Some were married to Indian women, others were civilized families of Makuráp, Jabotí or Tuparí, isolated from their tribal territories to the south and differing from their neighbours only in degree of identification with their ethnic origin. They lived in similar houses and utilized the same technology and essentially similar subsistence techniques. For both, the basic productive unit was the nuclear family, although the aboriginal rubber tapper usually had relatives in the area. Both were nominally Catholic. Rubber tappers looked down on their Indian neighbours and were quick to differentiate themselves from them. Intermarriage occurred only as a last resort, and such unions, especially with recently contacted groups like the Pacaa Nova, often did not last very long. The degree of contempt that rubber tappers, even Indian ones, have for their less "civilized" neighbours, is dramatically illustrated by the case of Chico, an acculturated Tuparí who worked for a seringalista on the Rio Pacaas Novas. Chico, isolated and needing a wife, had been forced to marry a Pacaa Nova from the Rio Negro region. The marriage lasted four years and produced two off-spring, but it finally broke up because of Chico's heavy drinking. When the woman returned to her kin on the Rio Negro, her three-year-old daughter refused to go, and informed her mother that she was not a *caboca* (in this case a local designation for a recently contacted Indian), but a person. Like Chico, the more acculturated Makuráp and Jabotí from the seringais on the Rio Branco went to great lengths to disassociate themselves from less civilized groups, creating a hierarchy on the basis of degree of acculturation.

These negative evaluations of the tribal Indian were not limited to the backwoodsmen, the rubber tappers, or peasants, but were also present among urban dwellers in the frontier zone. Brazilians had always viewed the Amazon interior as unoccupied territory, and the Indian as part of the wildlife of the forest. Among the local population, there was general agreement that indigenous groups did not deserve to occupy what they referred to as "some of the richest land in Brazil." Indians did not exploit their lands rationally and wasted the great natural resources available to them, and Indian resistance and defence of territory were interpreted as criminal acts that justified brutal retaliation and a call for their elimination in the name of progress.

In their uncontacted state, the Indians commanded fear for their fighting prowess but, once pacified and transferred to more accessible locations, they lost even that modicum of respect and became the despised "Indios mansos" or domesticated Indians. Although urban dwellers treated all rural folk with disdain, Indians were singled out for greater abuse. They were made the butt of jokes in the street, ignored, treated brusquely in stores, and exploited by nearly everyone. Abusive treatment of the Indian has been justified by their alleged "lack of the essentials of human-ness... Humans do not go naked like animals." The conviction that Indians are but beasts of the woods is a common theme, especially in the frontier zones of South America, and is expressed by many ranchers, farmers, rubber tappers, and prospectors, who compete with the Indian for land and resources. But it is also a theme taken up by those in the cities, who have a direct economic interest in the Indians' elimination.

Mineral Discoveries And Urban Growth

Although rubber prices and production continued to rise in the early 1950s, the rubber frontier did not experience the boom. Prices remained fairly low and were dominated by local demand. Increased interest in Rondônia, and new national and international attention came with the discovery in 1952 of high-quality cassiterite, or tin ore, in the granite masses of the Serra dos Pacaas Novas.

In 1959, cassiterite accounted for only 670,000 cruzeiros, of Rondônia's exports, while rubber led exports with a value of 483,606,000 cruzeiros. Brazil nuts followed at 77,899,000 cruzeiros. By 1958, Rondônia was exporting 20.56 tons of cassiterite, and by 1967 it had replaced rubber as Rondônia's chief export, with a value double that of rubber (IBGE Census 1970). It was estimated that Rondônia could yield five million tons of the metal, the equivalent of all known world reserves (Moreira da Rocha 1971:135).

In 1970, new government legislation prevented small prospectors who had flooded into the region from operating, and gave extraction rights to large companies "who could afford to extract the metal more efficiently." Larger companies have also always been more effective in pressuring the government to deal with the "Indian problem.." The discovery of cassiterite in 1952 meant increasing penetration into Pacaa Nova territory and a greater probability of hostile encounters. The growing importance of mining influenced the government's decision to proceed with "pacification." The opening of the highway linking Pôrto Velho and Cuiabá in 1960 and, the development that was bound to come with it, made it imperative that the Indian question be resolved.

The new surge of population growth after the low point of 1930 affected the urban centres most strongly. Although Guajará Mirim was elevated to the status of a city in 1928, and became the seat of a prelacy or frontier diocese two years later, it had only a few hundred inhabitants. By 1940, urban and suburban zones in the municipality of Guajará Mirim contained 1,977 people, or 32.5 percent of the inhabitants. That percentage rose to 37.4 percent in 1950, 43.6 percent in 1960, and 51.7 percent in 1970.

The former sleepy rural settlement began to be transformed into a thriving centre, the focus of all economic, bureaucratic, legal, religious, social, educational and medical services for the large hinterland, especially to the south of the city. Much of Guajará Mirim's growth came from the expansion of bureaucratic and professional services. The establishment of a frontier regiment reflected the government's increasing interest in its far west territory.

The townspeople, largely migrants from other urban centres, brought with them a desire for a faster, more modern lifestyle, and aspired to the services and cultural activities of cities to the east. A series of sports and social clubs provided the basis of social life and helped to define the individual's social status. Not inappropriately, the most exclusive club in Guajará Mirim was and is the Club Sirio-Libanese.

Few services extended beyond the limits of the city, and only a small number of upper- and middle-class urbanites had any knowledge or contact with the jungle beyond its borders. Bureaucrats, educators, and even the clergy were reluctant to put up with the isolation, hardships and primitive living conditions associated with the interior. They referred to the rustic inhabitants of the vast rural zones as *caboclos*, a term that summed up the ignorance, lack of sophistication, and crude manners of the peasants and rubber tappers. These, in turn, applied the same designation to the native population, with much the same meaning.

The traditional paternalistic system of the seringal served as the main link between the city and the interior. Seringalistas maintained their residences and conducted most of their business in Guajará Mirim. City influences filtered into the rural areas through a constant movement of peasants and rubber tappers in and out of the city. They occupied huts at the edge of the city or in the insalubrious zone close to the river. Sometimes they moved there to escape the isolation of the forest, to look for a wife, or merely to spend the rainy season with relatives. The young migrated to town in search of jobs, and some older rural dwellers spent their last years there with their grown-up children. The few professional and semi-professional fishermen in the area usually spent part of the year in town.

There was also a steady migration from the hinterland to urban centres. Some employment was usually available in construction, but most migrants performed odd jobs or were self-employed in transportation or sales. The major advantage of urban living was ready access to at least minimal medical care and education, and the social and spiritual services of the church. Some rural dwellers sent their children, especially their daughters, into town to be adopted by the family of their patron or by some other middle- or upper-class family. These children received some education, but were above all exploited as cheap domestic labour.

Protective Intervention

Within frontier society, relations between the Indians and civilizados were mediated by two "agencies of protective intervention" (Ribeiro 1970), the Indian Service and the religious missions.

The Indian Service emerged in 1910, following a controversy over government policy and action toward hostile native groups who stood in the path of settler expansion into the rich lands of the interior of São Paulo State. On the one hand, the settler representatives and the state government clamoured for a final military solution; on the other, a group of idealistic army officers, led by Mariano Cândido da Silva Rondon, pushed for a peaceful solution and for protection of Indian land and culture.

Rondon had seen the devastating effect of national expansion on indigenous people in Brazil's western frontier when he pioneered the building of a telegraph line. Stimulated by the positivist ideas of the period, he and his colleagues formulated a philosophy of coexistence, based on the right of native peoples to their own culture and their own lands. That philosophy became the basis of the Serviço de Proteção aos Índios (Indian Protection Service SPI). It expressed itself in a policy of peaceful contact and protection of Indian culture, combined with a gentle pressure towards integration with the national society.

In the interplay of national and regional economic interests, Rondon's oft-quoted philosophy was not translated into effective policy or action. The Service developed a highly successful technique for "pacification"; it brought hostile groups into peaceful relations with the expanding frontier, but was much less successful in protecting the Indian from the pressures of that frontier. Pacification tended to have disastrous consequences for the physical and cultural survival of tribal groups, and inevitably led to the loss of much of the land they had occupied. Rondon's philosophy and policies themselves stood in contradiction, the ideals of respect for Indian culture and support for the right of self-determination were not consistent with a policy of integration that made native groups dependent on the government and defined them as minors before the law. The same philosophical contradiction created a structural contradiction. As an agency of the dominant society, its policies and actions could not possibly run contrary to perceived national interest and expect to be successful.

The struggle by anthropologists and indigenists to persuade the government to establish an Indigenous Park for the Yanomamo of northern Brazil (Taylor 1979) provides a detailed example of what happens to plans perceived to be out of harmony with regional expansion policy. Even though legal mechanisms existed to provide land for the group, the possibility of activating them was remote.

Throughout its history, the Service was linked to ministries involved in national expansion and development. Even through its golden period under Rondon, the agency was constantly plagued by a shortage of funds and personnel. From the 1930s on, the idealists under Rondon were replaced by uncommitted bureaucrats, and the Service began to decline. The central administation increasingly lost contact with regional offices, and they, with local posts. Headquarters was hopelessly out of date and misinformed. For example, in the 1940s a post was established at Rio Riberão to pacify the Pacaa Nova; not only did it not bother to contact this group, it had very little information on their whereabouts or numbers. Even inspectors in Guajará Mirim seemed to have little idea of what went on at the posts in their area.

The presence of the Service had never been very strong in Rondônia. Law meant very little in these remote areas, and the seringalistas wielded the real economic, political, and even judicial power. The Service could rarely effectively oppose the local power structure. The fact that after 1930 most personnel of frontier posts were recruited locally, and shared local attitudes toward the Indians, made it unlikely that they would advocate or enforce policies in opposition to the interests of their neighbours, friends or compadres. There were some notable exceptions, but these could expect to be transferred out of the area because of complaints, charges and accusations brought against them by local economic elites.

Most Indian agents of the period had no real understanding of, or much fluency in, the language of their group. They lacked understanding of other cultures and problems of culture change, a situation which led Baldus (1960:258) to write that "they seem like surgeons who have never heard of anatomy, never had a scalpel in their hand. They ignore the body and soul of their wards, being neither doctors nor ethnologists." (Author's translation)

The harsh conditions of the frontier, without adequate food, shelter, or medical care, took their toll; combined with low salaries, they made bribery and corruption inevitable. In 1967, the Service was rocked by a scandal of major proportions. An in-house investigation resulted in a large number of officials from the local to the national level being accused of crimes ranging from cheating and stealing, to closing their eyes to, or actively cooperating in, the slaughter of Indians by ranchers, seringalistas, mining interests and real estate speculators. Before the cases came to court, the records were destroyed in a fire. Nevertheless the Service, totally discredited, was disbanded by the government and replaced in 1968 by the Fundação Nacional do Índio (FUNAI), a new organization associated with the Ministry of the Interior. Although FUNAI inherited much of the personnel of the Service, it recruited a team of well-educated young people, and trained them in both the social and the technical aspects of their role as directors of the agency's indigenous posts. The new agency also inherited the SPI's subordination to the interests of development; in this case, represented by the interests of the Ministry of the Interior. Lacking adequate resources or even the fundamental necessities for health and well-being, the young, idealistic officers in the field quickly became disillusioned. Some of the Indian posts were so isolated that a team from England's Aborigines Protection Society, invited to tour Brazil in 1971, were unable to find them (Brooks 1972). The Society reported, and my own experience confirms, that the new agents were unable to cope with the antagonism of the local population and the isolation. Most, rarely lasted over a year before asking to be transferred or making arrangements for their families to stay in the nearest town. Of course, once they had established a home, they naturally wanted to spend more time in town and away from the everyday affairs of the post. There were exceptions; I know of one dedicated agent who spent six consecutive years at his post. With the birth of his first child, however, he moved his wife into town, and later, when the child was ready for school, he requested a transfer to a more developed region of Brazil.

Because their stay in any given area was short, few agents mastered more than the fundamentals of the native language, and often had to rely on missionaries or marginal individuals for communication with their group. Most new agents had little experience or understanding of the conditions of the frontier zones, but were drawn into the Service by idealism, by the romance of working with tribal people. They found domesticated "tame" Indians lacking in glamour. In casual conversation, they liked to reminisce about their training days, when they visited such recently pacified groups as the Cintas Largas, who with their labrets, long hair and pride in their own culture still looked and acted like real Indians.

Even after the reorganization of 1968, the impact of the Indian agency was only limited to about half of Brazil's tribal societies. The rest had direct contact with the frontier, or were dependent on religious missions. In some cases, both FUNAI and the missions, especially evangelical foreign missions, worked with the same groups.

Missionization

Catholic mission enterprises in Brazil have always had close ties with the state. During the colonial era, they furthered state interests in the expansion and occupation of the vast interior forests. Since independence, the missions have had to rely more heavily on foreign priests: Italian and German Salesians and Jesuits, and, in Rondônia, French Franciscans. For purposes of missionization, the frontier territories are divided into prelacies under the control of religious orders, rather than the usual diocese controlled by secular priests. The designation reflects their emphasis on missionization and their pioneering character. Unlike the settlers, who questioned the essential humanity of Indians, the church accepted their human status from the beginning. They were merely pagans who had not been given the opportunity to accept the Christian God.

The Catholic Church in Brazil has always been part of the established order. In the frontier, where the state's presence is minimal, religious orders have controlled many public services usually reserved for the state, such as education, health, communication, transportation and the organization of cooperatives. Even foreign aid was channelled through the prelacies. In some areas (for example, the upper Rio Negro) efforts were concentrated on the indigenous population. By contrast, missionization was never primary within the Prelacy of Guajará Mirim, with its large population of rubber tappers and peasants; programmes for native people were combined with larger "development" projects.

The church generally accepted and collaborated with expansion into Indian territory. Its cooperation policy is manifest throughout the nineteenth-century colonial period, and is no less evident in the first half of the twentieth century. There is little doubt that the Prelacy of Guajará Mirim , for example, agreed with the settlement and exploitation of resources of the hinterland. The mission journal *Lettre d'Amazonie*, in a preface to a short article on the history of the Pacaa Nova pacification, states that "several expeditions which lasted five months were necessary to liberate definitively a zone rich in rubber, of the menace which paralyzed its economic development" (1965:12:4, author's translation).

During the 1930s and 1940s, the Prelacy was content to work with the rubber tappers and peasants. Priests visited the remote areas infrequently, to read mass and to bring the sacraments of baptism and marriage. Mass was read to even recently contacted Indian groups, but the padres did not exert much pressure for rapid conversion. They did not speak the local idiom and had little understanding of the culture of the tribal groups in the territory. Their one attempt to establish a mission among the tribes of the Guaporé ended in failure.

The Protestant missions, relative newcomers to the scene, are represented by fundamentalist mission societies like the New Tribes Missions and the Wycliffe Bible translators. Although they have recently begun to work with the local population, they are primarily set up to work with tribal groups. According to their own literature, they dedicate themselves "to the task of bringing God's Word to every tribe in its own tongue," and, in the process, to winning converts to the faith. They operate on the assumption that tribal groups are "living in an ancient world of superstition and fear" and that it is "evil and immorality which exudes from the tribal system."

To bring the "word" to tribal peoples, the mission organization has developed a very effective training programme based on the latest linguistic techniques. The method requires an understanding of language and culture; without this combination, translation would be impossible. The missionaries concentrate on individuals and stress personal salvation. They focus on potential leaders within the community, and work through them. As soon as a segment of the Bible is translated, the ability to read becomes the *sine qua non* of leadership among the converts. Since the missionaries' prestige is high, and they often control access to outside material goods, their support is essential for the emergence of leaders in the new context of dependence.

Although the Protestant missionaries provide some medical and economic assistance, their only real objective is spiritual — the evangelization of the Indian. They are governed by the conviction that all other problems can be reduced to spiritual ones. A missionary from Guajará Mirim expressed this quite clearly in assuring me that "once they (the Indians) have accepted Christ, all their other problems will be resolved.

The missionaries themselves are largely North American or European. They come from quite diverse backgrounds and from all walks of life, but have in common a profound personal experience of a God who came to them at a time of personal crisis and led them to the missionary vocation. In the rugged, lawless frontier with its gambling, drinking and loose morals, they set themselves apart through a rigorous, highly moral life-style; they tried to provide a model of Christian family life and to instill the values of individual achievement.

They work with tribal peoples on sufferance of the Indian Service. In their contract negotiations with the Service, they stress their linguistic and educational contributions and, in the 1960s, offered linguistic courses in Brasilia for FUNAI. They actively collaborate with the government, putting mission planes and radio transmitters at the service of FUNAI and the Ministry of the Interior. As Orlando Vilas Boas points out, "they never defend the Indian publicly or engage in any activity that might jeopardize their access to the region."

Out of eagerness to enter into contact with "heathen" groups, missionaries are likely to collaborate with seringalistas or other economic interests that are eager to bring about the pacification of tribal peoples. In the 1950s, they cooperated with seringalistas in the penetration of the Rio Pacaas Novas, and the pacification of the Oro nao, Oro eo, and Oro at.

The New Tribes missionaries made their first converts in 1968. Since that time, they have become very influential, not only as mediators with the outside world, but also in the internal affairs of the mission post. By constantly criticizing behavior that deviated from "Christian norms," they managed to suppress many of the outward expressions of Pacaa Nova culture and identity. And because of their defence of the Indian, they alienated the neighbouring Catholic civilizados, thereby increasing Indian reliance on the missionary society.

Rivalry between Protestants and Catholics became quite intense in the 1960s. The initial successes of the New Tribes Missions caused consternation in the Prelacy. Both sides had supporters within FUNAI and the local governments. During the pacification of the early sixties, armed clashes were only narrowly averted as each side tried to exclude the other. The Prelacy appealed to nationalist sentiment, labelling the New Tribes missionaries "Yankee agents" and raising suspicion as to the real reason for their presence. *Lettre d'Amazonie (1970:33:10)* refers to missionaries as "ethnologists, geologists and mineralogists, gold and diamond hunters masquerading as catechists," whose real reason for working in these remote areas was to exploit Brazil's natural riches and cheap Indian labour. In turn, the New Tribes Missions generally portrayed the padres as venal and corrupt, and their activities as detrimental to the Indians. The resultant back-biting and slanderous allegations were a source of confusion and bewilderment for the Pacaa Nova.

The conflict disrupted relations between the Indians at the respective missions and affected potential marital unions between the settlements, unions that were crucial for the survival of the Pacaa Nova as an ethnic unit. Sagarana, a Catholic mission founded in 1965, was particularly hard hit, since by 1970 it found itself with a serious shortage of marriageable females.

The Indian Service only added to the confusion; some agents opposed any kind of missionary work as disruptive to their tasks, while others sided with either the Catholics or the New Tribes Missions. In the Protestant settlements of Pitop, Dr Tanajura, and Rio Lage, the FUNAI personnel provided an alternative for Indian dissidents who rejected the influence of the missionaries. The degree of turbulence in each post was very much influenced by the relationship between the FUNAI agent and the New Tribes missionary. At Rio Negro-Ocaia, where the relationship was a good one, the settlement exhibited considerable solidarity and through cooperative enterprise made the post into a real social centre focused on religious gatherings rather than on traditional social forums. The weekly religious meetings held at the centre fostered the emergence of a new sense of community and a new leadership based on the ability to function in, and exploit, the new situation.

THE PACAA NOVA

The bands collectively referred to as Pacaa Nova first appear in the literature in 1798, where they are mentioned in their present location by Col. Ricardo Franco.

"Pacaas-Novos... on the river of that name, a tributary of the Mamoré, these are the nations who live on the western side of Serra dos Parecís and on the tributaries of the Guaporé (1857:244)".

It is possible that they were labelled differently by earlier expeditions since there is much variation and a great deal of confusion in terminology for ethnic groups contacted in the seventeenth and eighteenth centuries. Nothing is known of the Pacaa Nova's origin, and their mythology does not make reference to an earlier homeland. In fact, *"paticum"*, the place where souls go after death, is located in the waters of the Rio Pacaas Novas.

The Pacaa Nova are linguistically related to a number of "tribes" in the same region, such as the Jarú, Urupá, Huanyam, Moré, Itén, Cautário, the Chapacuran tribes further to the south and the Torá to the north (Mason 1950; Loukotka 1968). These groups, with the exception of the Moré and Itén, are now extinct.

On a map of Nova Luzitania published either in 1798 or 1804 (reprinted in Hugo 1959, Vol. 1:32), a tribe listed as Pacanoa appears on the left bank of the Mamoré. No other source confirms such a placing, and since the cartographer does not cite a source of reference it is possible the Pacanoa either are another group or were misplaced by the mapmaker. Passing reference is again made to them in 1823 by a missionary, Frei José Maria Macerato, who describes them as the nation living on the right shore of the river of the same name which flows into the Mamoré, as not being very brave, and as always avoiding contact with the traders from Pará (Hugo 1959:II:344). None of the explorers and scientific visitors during the early and middle part of the nineteenth century provides any further information. João Severiano da Fonseca, who travelled through the area in 1875-78 and left a detailed account, merely acknowledges their existence.

"The Pacaas-Novas or better Pacahas Novos, was the name of the tribe which inhabited its shores and perhaps still inhabits them" (Fonseca 1899:18).

No one seems to have contacted the Paaca Nova. Other late-nineteenth-century travellers (Keller (1868), Church (1870), Pinkas (1883), Palacios (1844-47) and Heath (1880)) who passed through the Mamoré – Madeira region make no reference to them; they may have been lumped with the Caripuna, Karitiana, or with the Jacaré, or other groups.

Given the lack of research in the area, the origin of the Paaca Nova remains obscure. Mason (1950:278) suggests that the northern Chapacuran groups, the Torá, Urupá, Jarú, and Pacaa Nova, moved into their present habitat in post-Colombian times, but does not discuss the sources that lead him to this conclusion. The problem of the origin and migration of native societies is complicated by the haphazard naming of ethnic units, especially groups not in contact with settlers, missionaries, traders, or travellers. They may be named by Indian guides or interpreters, who call them "outsiders" or "enemies," and the designation will vary according to the tribal origin of the guide or interpreter. As a result, completely unrelated units were classified together (as in the case of the Tapuia), or members of the same ethnic unit would be given different names.

This latter pattern seems more likely within the Madeira-Mamoré area, where an immense variety of labels were applied to the native groups of the region. In contrast, diverse groups would be called by the same name, especially if that name applied to a geographical location such as a river or mountain range. Small groups may have been referred to by the name of a local chief or influential man. Sometimes, the terms were arbitrary descriptive labels used by the Iberians, such as Cintas Largas or Bocas Negras (broad belts or black mouths). The name may have been in Spanish, Portuguese or an Indian language. If the term was elicited from a member of a group, it could be a personal name, a clan term, or a designation for some larger grouping. In the case of the Pacaa Nova, it could have been wari, the term for all the sub-groups, or Oro eo or Oro waram, the designation for the named groups, or could even have been the term for a residential unit. The latter might be based on a geographical location or the name of the most influential individual there. In the literature, the same term may be transcribed so differently as to be unrecognizable. For example, it is virtually impossible to equate many of the tribes mentioned by Snethlage (1937) with the groups referred to by Gonçalves da Fonseca (1875), Ricardo Franco (1857), or Severiano da Fonseca (1899).

Rubber tappers and local settlers are generally not interested in linguistic or cultural distinctions, indiscriminately naming whatever Indians they encounter. All this serves to confuse the ethno-historian and makes it extremely difficult if not impossible to sort out the smaller tribal groups, particularly if contact has been sporadic.

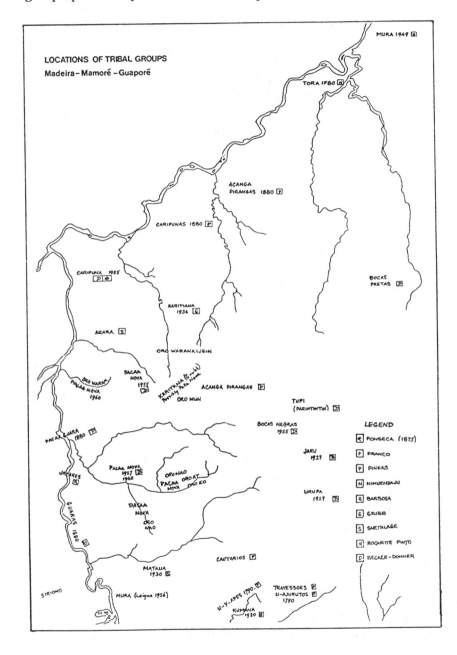

The preceding map shows the location of various ethnic units in the Madeira-Mamoré region, and demonstrates the problem historians face in attempting to identify the location and movement of "tribes". Only the best known, such as the Mura, the Mundurucú and the Parintintin, are consistently mentioned.

The Pacaa Nova speak a language that belongs to the Chapacuran stock, whose speakers, according to twentieth-century linguistic sources, occupy an area on both sides of the Guaporé stretching from the Cautário to the confluence of the Mamoré and continuing on the east side as far as the Rio Mutum Paraná. Leigue Castedo (1957:104), who lived and worked with the Moré in the 1930's, refers to the Cautário or "cau-ta-yo" who occupied the Brazilian shore in front of present day Puerto Moré as the Pacaa Nova. According to him the tribe in question spoke a language closely related to Moré, and that they practiced cannibalism. The evidence is inconclusive but if these were Pacaa Nova, it is possible that they retreated to the northeast as civilizado rubber gatherers and settlers moved into the region in the twentieth century.

The first documented clash between Pacaa Nova and civilizados occurred in 1910, when an exploration team of the Madeira-Mamoré Railway kidnapped several Indians from a village and exhibited them in Pôrto Velho (Lima Figuerêdo 1945:73). This, and similar hostile acts by rubber men, set the tone of contact between Pacaa Nova and civilizados for the next fifty years. Whether the Pacaa Nova were involved in attacks on the railroad crews is not definite, but in 1909 crews were ambushed at Chocolatal, an area inhabited by Pacaa Nova. Civilizado retaliation generally did not discriminate between ethnic groups — and any uncontacted Indians might suffer from reprisals. The rubber baron, Nicolas Suarez, who lost his brother to an "Indian attack", waged a merciless campaign against all groups in the area.

K. G. Grubb, a missionery observer who reported on Protestant missionary activity among South American lowland tribes in the 1920's, placed the Pacaa Nova in the area of the Rio Pacaas Novas, but said nothing further about them (Grubb 1927:117). The Rondon Commission survey makes only a brief reference to the Pacaa Nova (Barbosa 1948) and suggests a close linguistic relationship with the Jarú, Uomo, and Urupá. A short word-list from a Jarú informant at the Indian Service post of Rodolfo Miranda is cited as evidence. All this suggests that they assiduously avoided any contact with civilizados during that period.

Becker-Donner (1960), who surveyed the area earlier visited by Snethlage, wrote that in the 1920's "indios" that she identified as Pacaa

Nova came out to fish along the larger rivers, but retreated again and became hostile in the 1930's. She cites no sources for this, so one must assume that the information was probably gleaned from local informants.

Riveredo, a seringalista and ex-military man, reported widespread hostility between civilizados and Pacaa Nova from about 1927 on, with Indians responsible for the death of many rubber tappers (personal communications). He apparently visited a hostile village on the Rio Ouro Preto in 1929 in the company of two captured Pacaa Nova children. Enroute, he passed seven deserted villages, which, he said, were burned by Brazilian punitive expeditions. Attacks on railway crews and isolated rubbber workers continued in the 1930's. Mons (1939:3) reported that the Madeira-Mamoré Railway crossed areas inhabited by savage Indians. His report contains a photograph of three arrows, shown to him by the director of the railroad, that had been used in an attack on repair crews at kilometer 200. They have all the characteristics of Pacaa Nova projectiles, and Mons in fact identified the archers as Paca-ha Novas Indians who lived on the upper reaches of the Rio Pacaas Novas. An Indian Service official who was at the SPI post of Riberão for many years claimed that the most dangerous spot along the railway was the Igarapé Riberão, the territory of the Oro waramciyey, whom he considered the most warlike of the Pacaa Nova groups.

In 1937, a Pacaa Nova youth was shot in the hip and captured by a group of rubber men and taken to Pôrto Velho. He was then sent to the SPI post at Riberão, where the agent tried to enlist him in the pacification of his fellow tribesmen; before an expedition could leave he fled the post and was not heard of again.

After 1940, during the Batalha de Borracha, greater numbers of rubber tappers began to move up the Rio Pacaas Novas and Ouro Preto. A map produced in 1943 by the Rubber Development Corporation, Amazon Division (now in the railroad archives in Pôrto Velho) shows that rubber estates had reached the headwaters of those two rivers. The seringalista Lucindo, who was later involved in the pacification and who employed a number of Pacaa Nova in his seringal, moved into the region at that time. By the 1950's, the Rio Pacaas Novas was the most densely populated tributary of the Mamoré and Madeira, with 789 rubber tappers employed in its vicinity (Guerra 1953:231). Most of these rubber men were Nordestinos; their presence accounts for the increasing hostilities. Almost every year some rubber men as well as an unknown number of Indians were killed. Rubber tappers began to refuse to work in Pacaa Nova territory, and some seringais were abandoned. Railway crews also refused to service the line in some sectors, despite their being issued arms.

Increased hostilities in the 1950's threatened every major interest group in the territory. Seringalistas, already plagued by a labour shortage, watched their situation worsen as workers deserted some of the richest rubber areas. Profits aside, their very survival was at stake, since local business in Guajará Mirim was still predominantly linked with rubber production.

After the discovery of rich deposits of cassiterite at the headwaters of the Rio Pacaas Novas, prospectors and mineral companies began to show interest in Rondônia. The local civilizados were convinced that if development was to come, the Indian problem had to be settled. The seringalistas who were most directly affected had organized punitive raids since the 1930's, but had not been particularly successful against the highly mobile bands of Pacaa Nova. In the early 1950's, the seringalistas, unable to drive the Pacaa Nova out, began to negotiate with the New Tribes Missions in the hope of neutralizing the Indian threat through peaceful means. They volunteered some financing and supplied the site for an attraction post at the junction of the Rio Pacaas Novas and Ouro Preto. By 1954, New Tribes missionaries had staffed this site as well as a second post on the right bank of Igarapé Lage, an eastern tributary of the Madeira.

The pacification procedures followed the classic SPI model: presents of trade goods were left to lure the Indians out and to assure them of the missionaries' peaceful intentions. This method evolved into an exchange as the Pacaa Nova began to reciprocate with food. Finally, in 1956, face-to-face contact took place between small bands and the advance party of the New Tribes Mission.

Once contact had been established, small groups of Pacaa Nova began to come out frequently. In so doing, some of them contracted influenza. Unable to cope with the new disease, they asked the missionaries to help, and invited them to their villages to tend the sick. Fear of further outbreaks of disease, and the desire for knives and axes, finally led whole bands of fifteen to thirty people to seek out the missionaries and to establish part-time residence at the Rio Pacaas Novas post. By 1958, it became a permanent settlement and SPI post. Ferreira (1961), who visited it in the late 1950's, notes that at that time Indians were afflicted with influenza and that the two SPI functionaries of the post lacked the resources, especially food and medicines to help. Campos

(1964:59), a subsequent visitor, was told by an SPI doctor at the post that only 90 of the 400 who had originally come out were still alive. There is some disagreement over this figure of 400: Campos does not specify where it came from, and New Tribes informants claim that there were never that many in the region.

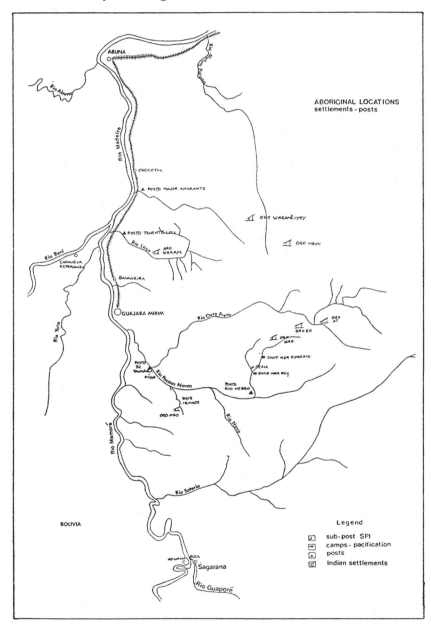

At the time of contact in the 1950's and 1960's, the Pacaa Nova occupied an area stretching from the Rio Pacaas Novas to the Rio Mutum Paraná in the north. Pacaa Nova sub-groups were concentrated in four clusters: the Oro nao of the lower Rio Pacaas Novas, Igarapé (creek) Dois Irmãos, and Rio Novo; the Oro eo, Oro at, and other Oro nao on the upper Rio Pacaas Novas and Rio Negro; the Oro waram around the Rio Lage; and the Oro waramciyey and Oro Mbun in the vicinity of the Igarapé Riberão and the Rio Mutum Paraná.

The Pacaa Nova contacted between 1954 and 1956 were the Oro nao (who today occupy the settlements of Pitop and Dois Irmãos, and Posto Dr. Tanajura). Pacification was limited to this isolated sub-group: they were not related to, nor did they have contact with, the Oro nao groups on the Rio Negro, or those on the adjacent Rio Lage.

Throughout the period 1959-60, the New Tribes Missions continued their efforts to pacify the still-hostile bands at the headwaters of the Rio Pacaas Novas. They built an advance post near the Rio Ocaia at this time, and made regular trips there.

Despite peaceful contacts with some of the bands, hostile encounters between Indians and Brazilians increased, especially in the area to the north. The rubber interests mounted a series of punitive raids, using Indians of other "tribal" groups as guides. They even tried to involve the military in these actions by claiming that a Brazilian army lieutenant, who disappeared in the jungle near Pôrto Velho in 1945, was alive and a captive of the Pacaa Nova. They hoped by this deception to mount an official rescue mission that would also drive the Indians out of the area.

The Pacaa Nova today freely talk about these raids, and still point to the scars on their bodies. Both New Tribes missionaries and Mason, an anthropoligist who worked with the Rio Pacaas Novas group, commented on the fact that Indians became agitated when planes passing overhead left vapour trails; an informant explained that a plane had once left a vapour trail or a trail of smoke that killed many wari. How many were killed cannot be determined, but the numbers are probably not very high, since the Pacaa Nova had the advantage of greater familiarity with the forest and were usually able to avoid encounters except on their own terms.

In the late 1950s, the situation came to a head. The whole territory seemed to be in an uproar. Suddenly Indians were seen everywhere, and every bush concealed savages waiting to pounce on unwary civilizados. The colonists at the Iata agricultural station (Presidente Dutra) increasingly feared an attack. Rumours circulated widely that Indians had been spotted on the very doorstep of Guajará Mirim. This crisis atmosphere was largely the creation of seringalistas, and was designed to bring about government action. Then, suddenly, the bogus threat became real: a former SPI official was killed near the Rio Lage, and on November 8, 1960, an attack took place that brought the tension to the breaking point and forced action. That day, on the road between Guajará Mirim and Presidente Dutra, a youth riding a bicycle was cut down by Indian arrows; his attackers cut off his arms and legs and fled with them.

Public opinion in Guajará Mirim was aroused to the extent that a posse was organized to do away with the Indian threat once and for all. To forestall this, the SPI and New Tribes missionaries dispatched a pacification party almost immediately. They were on hand when the Pacaa Nova struck again on the same road, this time wounding a Brazilian girl. They tracked the group to their encampment, but found it already deserted. In the clearing they found a giant hammock able to accommodate several men, placed in front of a large lean-to separated from the others by a palm screen. Abe Koop of the New Tribes Missions was later told that this was a *xijat* made especially for those who had slain an enemy. It separated the killers from the rest of the community while essential rituals were performed.

The pacification party stayed in the vicinity for several months, repeatedly returning to the village until they finally surprised a small group of Pacaa Nova who had returned to harvest some of their crops. The Indians immediately fled, but one woman who was unable to keep up was captured. Through interpreters from Posto Dr. Tanajura, they convinced the woman of their peaceful intentions and promised to make gifts of iron tools to anyone who would come out to make contact with them; they then released her. The next day all the inhabitants returned to the village to meet the pacification team. Once word of this peaceful contact spread, many more Oro waram came out, so many, in fact, that the SPI and the missionaries were unable to supply them with food and the promised presents. Within days, over two hundred Indians were struck down with colds and fever.

Rio Negro-Ocaia

Contact on the Rio Lage still left uncontacted hostile bands on the upper reaches of the Rio Pacaas Novas. The territorial government, pressured by local business interests, took matters into its own hands. The governor, Lt. Col. A. Mafra, appointed two special pacification agents, Fernando Cruz and Gilberto Gama, thereby bypassing the SPI hierarchy, and charged them with the task of pacifying the Pacaa Nova groups as quickly as possible.

Cruz arrived in Guajará Mirim in April 1961 under some confusion as to his role and authority. He claimed to have *carte blanche* for pacification of the Pacaa Nova from Janio Quadros, the new president of Brazil. He did not, however, have the necessary funds to undertake the enterprise and, under the circumstances, no one was willing to extend him credit. The Indian Service itself was already in debt and the town's businessmen were unwilling to risk further loans.

Cruz called a meeting of all seringalistas and major businessmen in Guajará Mirim and proposed that they finance the pacification, since peace in the area would benefit them most. He was turned down, but they agreed to reconsider as soon as he could demonstrate some progress in establishing contact. Cruz, acompanied by several Pacaa Nova from Posto Tanajura, subsequently left for the upper reaches of the Rio Pacaas Novas with Lucindo, a seringalista who had a large barracão at the headwaters of Rio Ocaia. On his return, Cruz claimed to have made brief contact with a small group of Pacaa Nova, but at another meeting was again refused funds. Everyone agreed that the Indians had to be pacified, but they wanted to see more results before agreeing to finance a larger expedition.

Cruz then offered his services to the New Tribes Mission but was also turned down since they had already set up an attraction post. As a final resort he turned for help to the Prelacy of Guajará Mirim. The priests, unhappy with the success of the New Tribes Mission, promised to provide some funds. An agreement was struck — in return for four million cruzeiros worth of merchandise given on credit by the Prelacy (*Lettre d'Amazonie* 1970:33:6), Cruz would "cooperate" with the Prelacy and help them establish a mission.

On May 19, as the expedition was about to depart, Cruz received a telegram from Regional Inspector Albérico of the Indian Service in Pôrto Velho, ordering him to remain in Guajará Mirim until the latter's arrival on May 22. The inspector, an evangelical Christian, had supported the New Tribes Mission and Cruz, and the padres feared that the expedition would be taken over by him and his New Tribes Mission friends. They decided to ignore the directive and left Guajará Mirim with an expedition of fifty people, including the mayor and one of the priests of the Prelacy (Padre Roberto); the bishop was to join the expedition later. At Posto Tanajura they picked up three families of "tame" Pacaa Nova who had earlier guided the New Tribes mission, and proceeded by launch to the mouth of the Rio Negro. From there, the expedition continued in smaller dugout canoes, and on May 26 established a base camp near the confluence of Rio Negro and Rio Ocaia.

Meanwhile, Albérico arrived in Guajará Mirim and, together with Major Duarte, the military medical officer, and Joe Moreno and Abe Koop of the New Tribes Mission, set out in pursuit. The two new missionaries were especially annoyed with Cruz, since they had already devoted some effort to establishing contact with the Rio Negro groups. According to various members of the Cruz expedition, Albérico met with a cool and even hostile reception, and was forced to abandon his take-over attempt. He withdrew with the intention of organizing an alternative pacification via the Rio Lage. To block him in this, Cruz sent his assistant, Gilberto Gama, and Padre Roberto to the Rio Lage with instructions to bring the Oro waram to the base camp at Ocaia. They brought out the Indians but were held up in Guajará Mirim for two days by the military, who accused Gama of dealing in drugs. Padre Roberto, writing in *Lettre d'Amazonie,* claims that thirty Indians came to Guajará Mirim, including a small number of men from the area of the Jaci Paraná who had come to visit their kinsmen on the Rio Lage.

The presence of "savage" Indians in the city brought out the curious among the townspeople. This sudden exposure infected some of the Indians with influenza. The afflicted fled immediately back to the Lage; the unaffected were brought to Ocaia to assist in the pacification effort.

On June 25-26, face-to-face contact was established. The Oro waram ran across three wild Pacaa Nova and, after some tense moments, persuaded them to come to the base camp. After much negotiation and many promises of gifts, they agreed to return with the remainder of their band. Excitement and fear characterized this preliminary encounter; neither side knew what to expect from the other. In the next few days, more Pacaa Nova came to the camp to gaze at their former enemies and pick up the material goods that were offered, but they also took away the deadly germs of influenza. Back in their encampments, they infected wives and brothers, daughters and sons, and soon, a major epidemic swept through the communities. After hearing of the epidemic, the members of the expedition visited the villages, but without medical supplies they could do little to stem the tide or relieve the suffering.

Padre Roberto, seeing the extent of the danger, immediately returned to Guajará Mirim for help. The requisite medical supplies were not available in Rondônia. He had to fly to São Paulo for them. When, after a long delay, the drugs finally arrived in Guajará Mirim, bureaucratic bumbling kept them there. When the relief supplies finally arrived at Ocaia after a delay of several months, most of the damage had been done. The medical team visited village after village of dead or dying Indians. In one settlement, all the Oro nao were dead; in another, ninety-two were sick. Within a three-month period, much of the population of the upper Rio Pacaas Novas had perished. No mortality figures are available, because of lack of accessibility and the dispersed nature of the various settlements.

The detailed events of the Rio Negro Ocaia pacification are difficult to reconstruct, since four or five different versions of these events had been put forth, depending on informants' affiliation with the Prelacy, with the New Tribes Missions, with the SPI, or with the territorial and municipal authorities. Each version reflects the interests of one of these organizations. The issue was further complicated by national political developments, in this case the unexpected resignation of the president of Brazil, and the replacement of the governor of Rondônia by new authorities who were unwilling to honour his commitment to the pacification effort.

During this second expedition, the alliance of Fernando Cruz and the padres fell apart. The Brazilian press, led by the major dailies of São Paulo and Rio de Janeiro, had by this time caught wind of the story and had described the plight of the Indians in graphic detail. The publicity called for action on the part of the Indian Service. Cruz, in an effort to shift the blame, ordered the Catholics out of the area. The SPI accused the Prelacy of responsibility for the many deaths, and prohibited their entry into Pacaa Nova territory. Still with the floodlights of publicity on him, Cruz ordered the expulsion of the New Tribes Missions. By this time, the story had become too big, and control of the pacification was turned over to another, more experienced and senior Indian Service official, who launched an investigation into the affair. His intervention merely added to the confusion and bad feelings, and the mutual recriminations did little to aid the survivors of the epidemic.

Rio Riberão

At this stage, the only area not pacified was the northern zone of the Oro mbun and Oro waramciyey. The SPI had constructed Post Major Amarante on the upper reaches of the Rio Riberão in the early 1940s, with the express purpose of bringing about peaceful relations with the Pacaa Nova. Several sporadic attempts to establish contact had been previously made, but in the 1950s the post served only the remnants of some of the Guaporé tribes, such as the Makuráp and Jabotí. One agent even forbade further overtures toward the Pacaa Nova.

In 1961, after the pacification on the Rio Lage and Rio Pacaas Novas, orders came from Pôrto Velho to proceed as quickly as possible with the pacification of the northern region. A team from the post, accompanied by some "tame" Oro nao from Posto Dr. Tanajura, made several forays into the upper reaches of the Rio Riberão, and finally came face-to-face with a group of seventy-four Oro waramciyey who had heard that peaceful contact had been established with their neighbours to the south. The group, after some negotiations with the guides, allowed itself to be taken to the post on the Rio Riberão. (SPI officials later claimed that these Oro waramciyey voluntarily left their villages because they feared attacks by seringalistas if they stayed in their own territory). News of the event spread rapidly and, within a short time, two hundred and eighty-six Oro waramciyey and Oro mbun descended on the post to "fraternize" with the agents of the SPI. Unfortunately, passengers of a weekly train that stopped at Posto Major Amarante also descended on the post to have a look at the famous Pacaa Nova who in the last ten years had acquired the reputation of being the scourge of the Madeira and Mamoré. This proved fatal; almost immediately the Indians contracted influenza. The most vivid impression of the episode was supplied by the post's Indian agent, José Dias, "a continuous roar of coughing that came from the Indian camp."

The tragedy on the Rio Pacaas Novas was now repeated: the SPI found itself unable to feed or provide medical care for these people. Its officials were usually trained in elementary first aid, but had neither the knowledge nor the medical supplies to deal with a major influenza epidemic, and despite the agent's daily trips to the agricultural colony at Iata, there was not enough food to meet even the basic needs of the Indians.

Just after the onset of the epidemic, a group of Oro mbun left Riberão and returned to the interior, not to be contacted again until 1969. Early that year, in a surprise ambush on the family of a rubber tapper, they killed three women. The SPI immediately dispatched a pacification team guided by several Oro mbun who claimed to have relatives with the hostile band, and led by an official who had participated in the Rio Pacaas Novas expedition. The pacification was accomplished quickly and easily. The group was brought to the post at Riberão, and later to a new Catholic mission settlement at the junction of the Mamoré and Guaporé where many of their kin were residing.

CULTURE

In these pages, the groups that make up the Pacaa Nova have been dealt with as one ethnic unit or "tribe." There is widespread confusion and arbitrariness in the nomenclature used for various kinds of indigenous groups, particularly in the use of the term "tribe." A lot of ink has been spilled in attempts to define "tribe," "band," or other such ethnic units, but in almost all of the literature two main defining elements emerge, the emic categorization of self-identification, and the etic identification of the anthropologist, based on language and culture. Historic precedent may be an influencing factor as well. Most definitions are based on a combination of these criteria. The groups referred to as Pacaa Nova by the surrounding Brazilian population all identify themselves as *wari*, in opposition to neighbouring and sometimes linguistically related groups such as the Moré, Huanyam, and Jarú, who are usually referred to as *wijam*, (literally, outsiders or enemies.) The six groups — Oro nao, the Oro eo, Oro at, Oro waram, Oro mbun, and Oro waramciyey, all of which I have dubbed "named groups" — consider themselves wari.

Conflicts among the wari are settled through fission, where one faction moves out to establish an independent settlement or to join another residential unit. Fighting among them is now limited to club fights *(papao)*, which are a highly regulated form of conflict resolution. Whether all groups accepted this form of conflict resolution in pre-pacification times is not clear. The New Tribes missionaries were told by some of their informants in the early years of contact that actual warfare between named groups had occurred in the past.

All of the Pacaa Nova speak closely related dialects. According to those who participated in the initial contact, native speakers would only require one or two days to adjust to the dialects of even the geographically most distant groups. Alan Mason (personal communication) differentiates two dialect groups, one that includes the Oro nao, Oro at, and Oro eo, with the other including the Oro waram, Oro waramciyey, and Oro mbun. The Protestant missionaries who worked with the Oro nao had some trouble understanding taped mythological material that I collected from the Oro waramciyey at Sagarana, but there seemed to be little problem in day-to-day communication between the two groups.

Geographical contiguity reinforced dialectical similarity. Only one area seems to have lost contact with the others, the Oro nao of the lower Rio Pacaas Novas and Igarapé Dois Irmãos were cut off by rubber tappers moving up the Rio Pacaas Novas and the Rio Ouro Preto. Among the others, there seems to have been some contact and visiting. A group of Oro mbun from the area of Rio Riberão were visiting the Oro waram at the Rio Lage at the time of pacification and another group of Oro mbun were found in the Rio Negro area in 1961. Contacts with neighbouring settlements were maintained by reciprocal visits, drinking feasts, and, in some cases, marriages. The Oro mbun in particular seem to have had contact with and been present in several areas.

All the groups referred to as Pacaa Nova had a similar culture. There were some differences in detail, such as mythology, style of singing, or type of wailing at sickness or death; but these are expectable ethnic markers among local groups. The overall impression is one of cultural homogeneity.

Aboriginal population figures are difficult to calculate because of the extensive ravages of diseases brought by the contacting expeditions. Estimates from those involved in the pacification range between one thousand five hundred and four thousand. The higher figure comes from one of the priests who participated in the contact on the upper reaches of the Rio Pacaas Novas, who claims to have visited twenty-two villages belonging to the Oro nao, Oro eo, and Oro at. He reports that some had populations as high as one hundred. A former seringalista and a former SPI functionary, both with extensive experience in the area prior to contact, confirm the existence of settlements of that size. However, it is also possible that the priest saw some of the same people at adjoining villages. The New Tribes missionaries claim that this was probably the case. Reports of the number of settlements also vary considerably; the seringalista Lucindo claims to have seen thirty-six villages in a survey he conducted a few years prior to pacification, but he was unable to give population figures, since the inhabitants fled at the approach of his party. In his report, he made no attempt to differentiate between seasonal camps and villages, and may also have counted deserted settlements.

Abraham Koop of the New Tribes Mission, who participated in the pacification of the Oro nao at Tanajura and had visited the Rio Negro before and after contact, places the total Pacaa Nova population at one thousand to fifteen hundred, with only four to five hundred on the Rio Negro. He also states that settlements had an average population of twenty to thirty, that the pattern was essentially one of small, nomadic groups, and that the large concentrations reported by the priests are the result of the abnormal conditions of contact.

Precise and verifiable figures are available only for Riberão, where two hundred and eighty-six Oro waramciyey and Oro mbun came to the post before disease began to seriously affect them. Between two and three hundred were contacted at the Rio Lage.

Named Groups

The Pacaa Nova as an ethnic group are made up of a number of previously mentioned localized groups. The downriver Oro nao were, at contact, located on the southern tributaries of the Rio Pacaas Novas, especially the Igarapé Dois Irmãos. A second group of unrelated Oro nao were found further to the northeast in the vicinity of the Rio Negro, the Rio Ocaia, and the upper reaches of the Rio Pacaas Novas. This latter group was the dominant group in its region and might have numbered as many as one thousand. Bands of Oro at and Oro eo inhabited the same general region and were intermarried with the Oro nao at the time of pacification. The Oro waram occupied the upper reaches of the Rio Lage and extended as far south as the Rio Bananeira. Most of the Oro mbun and Oro waramciyey roamed the area further to the north, from the Rio Riberão to the headwaters of the Rio Mutum Paraná. A seventh group called the Oro jowin were said to be found in the same region in the past. Apparently, they differed somewhat in their culture according to Oro nao informants; this difference led to misunderstandings and finally to warfare and their annihilation. A number of Oro nao and Oro mbun informants now living in Sagarana claim that their fathers were Oro jowin.

Named groups may at one time have been endogamous, but at contact the smaller groups were already intermarried with the larger ones. In Sagarana, which contained Pacaa Nova of all named groups, fifteen of seventeen marriages contracted before the establishment of the mission were with members of the same named group. The converse is true of unions that took place at the mission. Named group affiliation was in theory passed on through the mother, and informants stated that children always spoke the mother's dialect. In fact, however, such decisions are related to political factors. For example, at Sagarana an Oro nao with an Oro mbun wife, claimed that his child was Oro nao. Since his own father was an Oro waram, a small minority group in Sagarana,

I asked why he did not claim to belong to that group. He answered that he was Oro nao because his mother was Oro nao, and he refused to see the contradiction. He identified and lived with a group of Oro nao, and it was an advantage for the child to be affiliated with this large and powerful group.

The degree to which younger Pacaa Nova are aware of and influenced by the civilizado pattern of patrilineality in their responses to these kinds of questions is difficult to determine, but it was the Oro nao who had most contact. In everyday social interaction, named group affiliation seemed to exercise little influence on behaviour, it was appealed to only in times of crisis such as club fights where although kinship was the primary determinant of recruitment, named group solidarity might be called on if no immediate kinship existed.

The Settlement Group

Each pre-contact settlement or village was an autonomous social, economic and political unit. There were no regular multi-community institutions and no decision-making units beyond the settlement. The size of villages varied from three to five houses of five to ten meters each. Becker-Donner, who toured the area just prior to pacification, describes a deserted village with five such huts. Each contained a raised platform bed running almost the full length and width of the house; the beds were made of paxiuba boards fastened to a log frame with vines, and were covered with palm leaf mats. She estimates a population of about sixty, an average of twelve per house (1954:108). At one time, the settlements included a hut that functioned as sleeping quarters for the unmarried men. The presence of this hut raises the question of settlement size of an earlier period, before extensive pressure by rubber and mining interests made larger settlements too vulnerable; in fact, larger villages were reported in the Rio Negro region, a more isolated area that was not as exposed to the attacks of rubber tappers.

The important functional unit in day-to-day activities was the settlement group. It was the predominant economic, social and political unit, and consisted of a minimum of fifteen to thirty individuals. In more remote areas several such units may have lived together or in close proximity, and the total population of the settlement may have approached eighty or ninety. The group usually clustered around one or several sets of siblings; it was flexible, and nuclear families moved freely, joining any settlement in which they had kin ties on either the male or the female side. Residential preference seemed to be largely dictated by circumstances, and rules were loose enough to accommodate different arrangements. This set of siblings and associated kin was the primary unit of cooperation and sharing, although expectations of reciprocity were also held by other members of the settlement.

Pacaa Nova family at Rio Negro - Ocaia.

The band of Oro mbun at Sagarana, which was pacified in 1969, is an example of such an "aboriginal" settlement group. It consisted of thirty individuals, members of two family groups linked by marriage bonds, with a core of two sets of intermarried siblings.

Subsistence activities were closely related to the seasonal variations of the environment. Although the Paaca Nova are basically horticultural and practice slash-and-burn agriculture, an increasingly important percentage of their diet was provided through hunting, fishing and foraging, especially during periods of intensive conflict with rubber tappers, when mobility was of prime importance. At such times villages were moved frequently, with only small groups returning to harvest the crops.

Members of the Oro mbun group pacified in 1969.

Mason, who worked with the Oro nao, distinguishes patterns of subsistence according to the two main seasons. Dry season activities are characterized by a tendency toward "inhabitation," in contrast to the rainy season where activities that require mobility predominate. The dry season begins in May or June and runs into September or October. Between these months the forest is cleared. Sites are selected on the basis of soil and access to water. Locations on smaller streams are preferred and the larger rivers are avoided, although the Indians sometimes fish them. They do not have watercraft and usually fish with bow and arrow from the shore. Fish are also caught with hook and line in the smaller streams, or by hand in very shallow creeks. During very low water levels, parts of streams are dammed up and poisonous vines are pounded in the water to kill the fish.

Hunting, considered the most prestigious activity, is reserved for men, and takes place all year. Much enthusiasm accompanies preparations for the hunt, and hunting stories are retold for months after to anyone willing to listen. Expeditions may be organized by one hunter or may bring together as many as a dozen men, and involve absences from the settlement for up to two weeks. On longer hunting trips, which usually take place during the rainy season, women and children accompany the party and small temporary camps are set up. The greatest excitement is generated at the sighting of peccaries, which run in herds. Meat is divided among kin, with special obligations to the hunter's parents-in-law. Success in hunting gives a man prestige and an opportunity to display the culture's most valued trait — generosity, while at the same time building up his credit for future reciprocity. The killing of larger game bestows more prestige, but most meat comes from monkeys, birds and a host of smaller animals.

Foraging, largely a women's activity, has little prestige attached to it but does provide a large, varied, and reliable food supply year round, as well as occasional delicacies such as honey or palm grubs.

Planting takes place at the beginning of the rainy season. When clouds begin to gather, the new dry clearings are torched, and corn, manioc and sweet potatoes are planted. The timing of the burn is important; ideally, it takes place just prior to the first rains, which provide the initial moisture for the germination of the seeds. The harvest begins in January and extends through the early part of the dry season, although manioc may be left in the ground for much longer.

According to both civilizado and native informants, the traditional environment was rich in fish and game. These, combined with foraging and agriculture provided the Paaca Nova with a varied and abundant diet. They view the period before contact as a "golden age," in contrast to the time when rubber gatherers cut their trails and began the cycle of anxiety, fear and violence.

The social world of the Pacaa Nova is delineated by kinship, which determines residence, marriage, cooperation, sharing, political support, and assistance in cases of conflict. It provides a framework of possible social choices; within that framework, an individual has some basic obligations to his immediate kin, but beyond that he may choose to emphasize or to downplay certain links. Certainly there are norms and expectations, but other political and economic considerations can play an important part.

The wari consider themselves to be in a universe of kin; most of my informants at Sagarana were able to give me kinship terms for all members of the village, even those for whom they could trace no geneological link. Denial of any kinship relation at Sagarana was limited to the Oro nao from Dois Irmãos, who had neither consanguines or affines among the other named groups and who felt isolated at the mission. By contrast, the others in Sagarana included the Oro nao in their terminological system. It seems likely that in so doing they were stressing general wari solidarity, whereas informants from Dois Irmãos were emphasizing their isolation and lack of close functional kin. To what degree current usage reflects the depopulation, subsequent resettlement and more extensive contact among named groups is hard to determine, but there is no doubt that there has been considerable change. Sagarana, especially with its mix of people from all areas, is most subject to change and compromise.

Because intermarriage has taken place between families for several generations and people stand in multiple relations to each other, it is not unusual for individuals to disagree on their relationship. Responses about kin relations tended to vary according to the timing and context of the question, and reflected an individual's desire to stress belonging or, alternately, to deny responsibility. For example, in cases of club fights kinship might be denied, but at a later date the same individual could claim a kin tie in order to share in the distribution of meat.

The world of kin is structured by degrees of closeness, bilaterally and by marriage restrictions. There are basically three varieties of wari. The first comprises "our relatives," the people one cannot marry and the ones an individual would call upon for help: grandparents, parents' siblings, siblings, and all parallel and first cross cousins and their children. Because of named group endogamy, these were the people who lived in the same area. The second group of kin are "those we don't know," or "those who live in the other settlement," or "those who live on the other side of the river." These are the people with whom marriage is permitted and preferred. The third group are wari who are not kin but are also potential spouses, or at least became potential spouses after the pacification team had established links between groups.

Early missionary descriptions and data collected among the Oro nao (Mason 1976) and at Sagarana indicate that marriage took place with members of nearby settlements along established patterns of marital exchange. The existence of such exchange between two groups is verified by data from Sagarana, and was brought to my attention when young people who chose to ignore tradition and marry outside this network became the object of criticism and gossip. The traditional patterns were reaffirmed by joint, social, ritual events such as the chicha feast.

The confused situation after contact and the social collapse that ensued make it difficult to discern any pattern of post-marital residence.

Certainly, it is futile to try to do so with contemporary data. Residence is now, and probably was in the past, flexible and subject to economic and political considerations. Fathers were reluctant to part with their daughters, and a suitor was expected to do bride-service for his prospective father-in-law, providing meat for his household and helping in the gardens. In some cases a husband might be joined by an unmarried younger brother, or even a married brother and his family; after the death of the older generation, this group of males become the nucleus of the settlement. The norm was patrilocality or virilocality, but a wife, even after she had left her father's household, was often successful in persuading her husband to spend some time with her relatives. When a couple visited another village where both had close kin they tended to stay with the wife's relatives.

Residential groups are made up of a core of siblings and their spouses and children. The size of the group often depends on the presence of an individual who is capable of influencing everyone and is able to draw other, less closely related individuals to the group.

Leadership among native groups has always confused Brazilians, who have European expectations that leaders have a distinct status and role. The Indian Service and members of the Rio Negro pacification team talk of chiefs, and refer to them as *dramaticon* (a term meaning male organ). It was claimed that these were "obeyed" on occasion by entire named groups. One of the padres involved in the pacification refers to a chief who was acknowledged by all of the Rio Negro settlements. There is no evidence from the Pacaa Nova themselves that such leaders existed and it seems more probable that they were a creation of the Brazilians, who are conditioned by their own culture to expect leaders. Individuals identified as chiefs were usually well-known, prestigious family heads with large numbers of kin, whose influence depended solely on persuasion but who had no real authority outside their own household. Such individuals may have acted more decisively in crisis situations or, at most, become spokesmen for the more reticent. But they could hardly be called chiefs in the usual sense of that word; they held no institutionalized position and had no right to exercise coercive power. The same pattern holds for the Moré, a linguistically related tribe on the Guaporé-Mamoré junction (Leigue Castedo 1957:34) and for the Nambicuara (Price 1981)

In the pre-pacification period, the extended family group clustered around and was held together by the senior male member, as long as he was still physically active. His influence and prestige depended on his personal charisma, the size of his immediate kin group, his prowess as a hunter, his generosity and ability to organize festive activities, his ritual knowledge, or his power as a shaman. He exercised some authority over his sons, younger brothers, cousins, and sons-in-law, but they might leave at any time and join another residential group in which they had kin. The most prestigious men at Sagarana were in the prime of life; with advancing age, men generally lost prestige unless they had strong supernatural powers. That old age was not valued is indicated by the term for old (hurun), which also means ugly. During the crisis period, just prior to contact, there are stories of old people being left in the woods to die when they were no longer able to keep up, but such behaviour seems to be related to the abnormal conditions at pacification, when rapid movement was essential to escape the guns of the seringalistas.

The most powerful family head at Sagarana was Paleto. His position of influence was somewhat extraordinary according to all my civilizado and Indian informants. He was a man of middle age, capable and diligent as a hunter and farmer. His knowledge of traditional mythology and ritual was unsurpassed, but it was primarily his reputation for supernatural power that accounted for his status. He drew a large number of younger men to his settlement and he initiated two of the three chicha feasts held during my stay in the field. Members from his group all indicated that it was he who "ordered" the chicha to be made. (I suspect that their comments and terminology partly derive from their contact with Brazilian society, where people order things to be done, and that Paleto's role was not much more than that of initiator.) When he moved out of the mission settlement, his brother and family and four younger men and their families moved with him.

Social control was exercised through the informal mechanism of social pressure, and criticism played a major role in enforcing cooperative behaviour. Sociability and conformity were valued and aggressive behaviour was sanctioned by the whole community. The major cause of conflict were sexual rivalry and marital disagreements. Men were extremely jealous; even coincidental encounters in the forest between a man and a married woman could result in accusations of adultery. Wives who felt abused by their husbands often returned to their kin, who in turn might seek redress from their in-laws. The New Tribes missionaries report an incident where the sister of a woman who had been beaten by her husband continued to call for a club fight and to demand that her brothers punish the man despite the fact that the married couple had settled their differences and wanted no outside interference. Common relatives acted as mediators when tempers flared, but often confrontation escalated into club fights.

Club fights, a highly regulated form of conflict among the wari, provided an occasion for the release of pent-up aggression through outbursts of verbal and physical violence. The usually calm and controlled Pacaa Nova vented all of their grievances and frustrations on these occasions, but since the fight was strictly controlled by non-combatants, who stopped the fight once a man was down, fatalities were rare. The clubs used were called *temem*, the word for bow, and if the fight took place on the spur of the moment, unstrung bows were actually used. Otherwise, heavier clubs with sharper edges were prepared. Blows were aimed at head and shoulders in order to make the blood flow; it was the spilling of blood that resolved the issue and allowed people to return to their normal social lives. To end hostilities, one of the principals might challenge his opponent to strike him on the head, without retaliating. In very serious cases, "referees" often lost control of the fighting, and serious injuries could result. In such cases one of the parties would have to leave the village.

Club fight at Sagarana 1970.

Woman attempting to halt the fight.

The flow of blood resolves the issue.

Religion

The world of the wari was full of spirits, many of whom could in some circumstances be harmful to people. To ward off potential evil, each individual must follow a strict code of conduct that involves food taboos, prescribed rituals, and avoidance of certain activities, especially during critical times such as pregnancy. The killing of animals, for example, had to be followed by a series of protective rituals designed to appease the spirits and cleanse the killer. Pacaa Nova wailed over game or fish in order to propitiate the spirit. The most serious killing is of humans, which makes the killer unfit to live in human society until a purifying ritual is performed. For example, after killing a fifteen-year-old boy who was bicycling on the outskirts of Guajará Mirim, the killers returned to the village where they consumed part of the body. They were subsequently restricted to a large hammock specially constructed for this purpose, and were isolated for several days. Women could not look at them and food had to be passed through the screen. Because the killing of humans had such potential for spiritual harm to one's family as well as oneself, usually younger, unmarried men took part in raids. Failure to follow prescriptions and taboos harms those least able to protect themselves; young children, mothers and pregnant women had to be specially careful not to eat certain types of game and fish. Details of food taboos and behavioral prescriptions vary according to named groups. Illnesses among young children are usually attributed to the spirits of tabooed animals, and relatives often blame the parents for carelessness in that respect. The missionaries at Posto Dr.Tanajura record an instance when such accusations almost led to a club fight.

Like animals, and even some plants, humans have a soul or spirit that is conceived of as a miniature person. The killing of this soul can cause a person's death. (The Pacaa Nova describe several ways in which enemy shamans can capture or trap a person's spirit and cause that person to sicken and die.) This spirit or soul wanders during sleep and is susceptible at that time. Once the soul has been killed, the victim will die within several days. In order to regain a soul, which goes to *paticum*, an afterworld thought to be located in the Rio Pacaas Novas, the body must be consumed by relatives and the bones burned and buried.

It was this custom that made headlines and accounts for some of the notoriety of the Pacaa Nova in Brazil. The leader of the pacification team on the Rio Negro photographed a cannibalistic scene involving the eating of a child, and sold it to a leading Brazilian weekly. Fortunately, publication was stopped when the Indian Service and Brazilian anthropologists intervened. Stories of this nature are sensationalized in the Brazilian press and are rarely placed within the context of the culture. They serve the interests of those who wish to eliminate native people in order to remove barriers to the exploitation of their lands.

The Pacaa Nova also speak of another spiritual entity which appears to be a reincarnation of the flesh; it has the appearance of a person long dead, with no hair, a bulging stomach, and deeply sunken eyes. I was not able to determine whether this in fact was the physical manifestation of a dead person whose flesh had not been eaten, since my informants were extremely reluctant to talk about former cannibalistic practices.

Data gathered by the New Tribes Mission during the early contact period and from interviews in post-pacification times emphasize the importance of shamanism and sorcery in daily life. Since most illnesses and deaths were directly attributed to sorcery practiced by members of other named groups, or to the effects of animal spirits, shamans were called in such instances to determine the exact cause of the malady. The two main causes were the killing of the victim's soul *(jamixi)* by an enemy, or the breaking of a food taboo. In the latter case, it was the soul of the animal eaten by the parents that caused sickness in children. The shaman would divine the cause through trance and communication with his guardian spirit, identify the perpetrator, and then attempt to cure the patient. Curing involved the passing of hands over the patient to find the offending spirit, which was then sucked out of the body and buried or thrown away. The harm-inflicting material was symbolized in some tangible form, a feather, seeds, a few hairs, or a fishbone.

Individuals became shamans through an actual or mystical encounter with an animal, during which they received the spirit of that animal. Such encounters were usually preceded by a period of emotional or physical crisis; in one case it was a serious illness, and in another, an encounter with a jaguar that mauled and almost killed the man. The spirit of that animal subsequently served as the latter's guardian and helper. In two cases, men went into the Brazilian rubber camps, drank cachaça (a type of cane alcohol), became very sick and lost a lot of weight, then returned to their settlements as shamans.

The most important shaman in the Rio Negro was left a cripple after his spirit encounter. His guardian spirit was the pig and he was said to "walk with pigs." He periodically had seizures, at which time his spirit communicated with him. During one of these seizures, while in the presence of several missionaries, he sent hunters to a site close to the village and told them to kill the pigs there. They encountered a herd of peccarry and killed eight of them. In some cases, sons of shamans inherit the predisposition to go into trance even if they do not wish to follow in their father's footsteps. The New Tribes missionaries likened some of the "seizures" they observed to minor epileptic fits. If the diagnosis is apt, it would account for the heritability of shamanic dispositions.

A number of communal ritual activities are still practiced by the Indians at Sagarana. The most important of these is a drinking feast, but there are also a number of other occasions such as the emergence of the new moon, when the community holds all night-singing sessions. Communal ritual activity serves a variety of important social functions, from bringing related settlement groups together to reaffirming social relationships. The most complex ritual is the drinking feast, or chicha feast, which is celebrated after the harvest in the early part of the dry season. I observed several chicha feasts during my fieldwork, but found that they were but shadows of their former selves. The description that follows is taken from the records of a missionary who observed a feast that took place in mid-August 1964 at the settlement of Dois Irmãos.

> The visitors from the Rio Negro arrived slowly at Dois Irmãos. They threw up a small palmshelter midway between the port and the settlement. There they prepared themselves for entering the village. One of the men wore a braided hat covered with down and all of them carried little three-cornered baskets (coc) on their backs; these were decorated with macaw feathers, monkey tails, or bird's heads. All of the men were painted with black genipapa. They entered playing large bamboo horns with a small gourd attached to the far end. They would keep this up until they were invited by the hosts to drink chicha or maize beer. While they were playing they called out to the women and tried to make different ones come forward but they refused. Finally a man painted with jaguar spots bounded out on all fours from among the visitors. His antics made everyone laugh and several women teased him. Finally one of them pointed a gun and pretended to shoot him and he rolled over and played dead. The

men from the Negro then went over to the men's house and sat on the raised platform where chicha was brought to them. The drink, stored in a large hollow log set vertically into the ground, had been made two months before. The men drank huge quantities and after a short time had to empty their stomachs by vomiting so that they could continue to drink.

The women from the Negro now came into the village and sat in a row in front of the men's house. Their men lined up in front of them leaning on large bamboo sticks. As the women began to sing the men started to pound the ground with these and step back and forth at a fast rate. One of the hosts carrying the short stick used to play the hollowed-out log drum, moved down the line of women holding the stick in front of each one. As he did this the other men of his group began to beat him on the back as if they were trying to chase him away. Several informants later told the missionaries that he was pretending to have sexual relations with the women and that the ones who were beating him were telling him to stop.

While this was going on and several other men went down the line of women, the visiting men continued to drink and vomit. Several men were begining to totter. One man sat down but one of the hosts blew into his ear and he revived enough to drink some more chicha. Another man looked like he was getting stiff. The hosts continued to blow into the drinkers' ears and give them more chicha. All of the Negro men were getting a little wobbly at this stage and the women were holding some of them up. Several men were still going strong.

One of the men collapsed and several men from Dois Irmãos carried him off and began to take off his clothing. As he lay, he was grinding his mouth until blood started to run from it. All the people around commented loudly that he had died, that he was killed. He was groaning and grinding his teeth and then suddenly he went stiff with his arm out straight. They took him over to the platform to lie down, saying that he had died and that tomorrow they would put water on his face and he would wake up. Another man began to run wild and started to shake with what looked like convulsions. He seemed to be getting unmanageable but several men held him down and another held his hands over his eyes. That seemed to calm him but after a while he began to tear around again. Another man was stiff and several men tried to loosen him. As he loosened up they gave him some more chicha and continued to blow into his ear. Several men passed out and were sleeping without being stiff. Apparently those with convulsions did not die. Only those who bled from the mouth died.

During all of this the women from the Negro continued to sing. By mid-morning all of the drinkers were sleeping. Only two of the group had died, the rest were either drunk or worn out.

The hosts were now heating water and when it was prepared they began to work on the stiffened joints of the two who had died. They worked the joints back and forth and began to splash water on the right leg, the left, the arms, body, and back, and finally water was thrown in their faces. They came to with a jerk and started to throw themselves around. Everyone was laughing now as some of the men tried to hold them down. Only those who had died were given this treatment.

The women from the Negro were still sitting in a row but were now singing a different type of song and both men and women from Dois Irmãos were watching them. The men began to line up in front of them and, stomping their bamboo poles on the ground, they repeated the dance that the men from the Negro had performed. The young unmarried men ran down the line of women with their drumsticks and placed them between the women's legs while others pursued them and beat them on the back. They repeated this several times and interspersed it with playing the log drums (pana). The women kept singing and beating a small rubber-covered drum which they passed around.

*Hosts bringing chicha to visiting group
Sagarana 1970.*

Chicha feast at Sagarana 1970

The feast well under way.

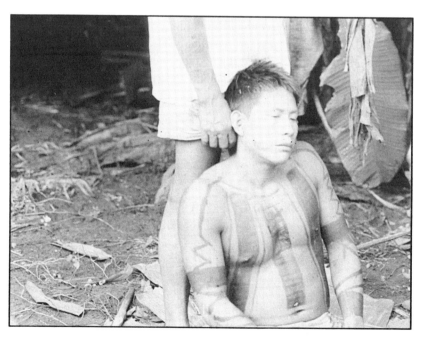

Participant about to "die".

> After the women stopped the men started to dance
> again, stamping the poles and rapidly moving back-
> ward and forward and loudly singing a song. They
> ended the song with loud yells.

The next feast would take place on the Rio Negro when the new corn came in, and the present hosts would be the guests.

The chicha feast required reciprocity and thus served to maintain social relations between neighbouring groups. The feast at Dois Irmãos provided an occasion for the affirmation of social and cultural ties between two distinct groups who had only established contact after pacification in 1961. After the epidemics, men from Dois Irmãos had gone to the Rio Negro and married women from there. The ambiguity of the affinal relationship was symbolically expressed by the ritual of the feast. The act of placing the drumstick between the legs of the Rio Negro women was clearly identified with sexual relations, and the symbolic blows administered to the dancer by the other men from the village, were meant to make him stop. They appear to represent the social control and formality that accompanies marriage between groups — the cultural harnessing of sex.

According to the Pacaa Nova, the drinking of such vast quantities has as its ultimate objective the achievement of a state of trance during which the drinker sees *jam*, spirits that according to informants help them kill their enemies. Since in the last twenty to thirty years these enemies were civilizados, the Pacaa Nova are understandably reluctant to talk about the *jam*.

POST-CONTACT CHANGES

Within months of pacification well over half of the Pacaa Nova had died of diseases brought in by the contacting expeditions. Most died even before members of the pacification team had reached all the settlements. Only five hundred or so survived. Exactly how many perished depends on which population estimates one accepts. All agree that a great many died; figures range between 65% and 80% of the pre-contact population. In Riberão, twenty-eight died of influenza two years later, and in 1970 another twenty died during a measles epidemic at Sagarana. Such a dramatic decline is not unusual for tropical forest groups and is well-documented by demographers and historians. In Rondônia as a whole, this is merely one incident in a history of tribal extinction and population decline.

The effects of a large-scale epidemic are similar to those of major disasters, where those affected go into a state of shock. Centrewall (1968:80) observed that during an epidemic crisis among the Yanomamo, community structure and function were lost, and healthy members abandoned the sick. An analogue among the Pacaa Nova, reported by Richard Sollis of the New Tribes Missions (personal communication), was women's refusal to nurse orphans. Ethnohistorians report similar disorientation and shock during epidemics among North American Indians (Ray 1974: 105: 106).

The mortality rates are extremely high; the effect on the social organization is equally dramatic. Neel (1971:578) who witnessed an epidemic, writes: "When an entire Indian village goes down with the disease there is a total collapse of daily life. In the tropics febrile individuals dehydrate rather rapidly if there is no one to bring them water... Infants are nursed till three years of age or over... You can imagine their plight when not only do they have measles but so do their mothers, with a drastic reduction of her milk supply and inability to care for her child."

Memories of experiences with the white man's diseases only increase levels of fear during an epidemic. Those affected are resigned to dying and this prejudices their chance for survival. During a 1970 epidemic at Sagarana, the afflicted felt they were as good as dead, even though death is frequently not the result of the disease itself, but of later complications. Most of the Sagarana fatalities survived the initial measles but succumbed to broncho-pneumonia or dehydration.

Studies show that the availability of medical care is crucial for survival. Epidemics documented by Nutels, an Indian Service doctor, indicate a mortality rate of 26.8% for those who could not be treated in time as opposed to 9.6% for those treated (1968:115).

The sudden shock of the epidemics and the inability of traditional shamans to cope with them produce a dependence on Western medicine and act as a strong incentive to live in the vicinity of the mission, SPI post, or centers of Brazilian settlement, especially for families with young children. Dependence was particularly strong during the early years of the post-pacification period, because those Pacaa Nova who had lost close relatives did not plant gardens and so had to rely almost entirely on the posts.

For a number of years families ceased to have children. This phenomenon is not exclusive to the Pacaa Nova; it has also occurred among some of the southern Guaporé groups such as the Cabishi, and seems to be related to the psychological impact of contact and the trauma of epidemics. From about 1965 on, the population again increased; by 1970 the largest age group was below the age of five.

The overall health of the Pacaa Nova altered rapidly with contact. Not only were they continuously exposed to new influenza and measles infections, but were now also exposed to parasitic ailments resulting from the unsanitary conditions of the settlements. The new villages grew larger and became permanent fixtures of the environment. Chicken, pigs and other domesticated animals were introduced, adding to the concentration of garbage, feces, pests and various pathogens. The concentration of people along the larger rivers where mosquitos are much more numerous increased the incidence of malaria, a disease that was virtually unknown in the Pacaa Nova's upriver settlements. Susceptibility to disease further increased with the deterioration of their diet (especially the decrease in protein intake that accompanied greater reliance on agriculture and the decline in game). Finally, the introduction of clothing complicated the problem of hygiene, since garments were initially worn until they fell off the wearer's back. Personal hygiene was also affected when many of the Indians refused to bathe while in the presence of outsiders, once they became aware of civilizado attitudes towards nudity.

The epidemics also had important repercussions and created irreversible changes in social organization. Two named groups, the Oro at and Oro eo, were almost wiped out. Others lost a large proportion of their population. Preferential marriages and ties between groups could no longer be maintained, and the loss of marital partners necessitated new arrangements. These adjustments were accompanied by frequent fighting. In the early days at Sagarana, club fights were almost a daily occurence, and most of them involved disputes over women. Several older men who had polygamous unions lost one of their wives to younger men. In the hardest hit villages, individuals lost virtually all of their kin and experienced great difficulty in adapting to new groups consisting primarily of strangers. Some children without kin became dependent on outsiders and alienated from their own people.

In the immediate post-pacification period, having the feared Paaca Nova as visitors was regarded as a novelty by the surrounding population. Some Pacaa Nova became quite friendly with people along the river, and began to hang around rubber encampments in the area. Initially they were encouraged and offered food or presents. Becker-Donner (1960) writes that they became accustomed to receiving presents without being expected to reciprocate. The Pacaa Nova were overwhelmed by this sudden hospitality and freedom to travel in areas where they had formerly not dared to set foot, and optimism and curiosity characterized that early period. Aspects of the traditional culture, especially material elements, were readily discarded in favour of the new manufactured goods. Brazilian dress and behavioural patterns were copied in an effort to identify with civilizados. So widespread were these efforts that Becker-Donner was astonished by the rapid acceptance of the new elements and the loss of the old among the Oro nao of Posto Dr. Tanajura.

Predictably, this phase was of short duration. As in other similar contact situations (DaMatta 1982:2), well-established stereotypes and patterns of domination in inter-ethnic relations soon reappeared. Within a few months, the civilizados no longer welcomed groups of Indian visitors. The presents stopped; the civilizados began to demand payment in the form of labour or produce.

The most decisive event for the future development of the Pacaa Nova was their removal from scattered locations at the headwaters of the Rio Pacaas Novas, Rio Lage and Rio Riberão for resettlement in communities closer to Guajará Mirim where they could be controlled by missionaries and SPI officials. The move, once accomplished, proved to be irrevocable, and destroyed the Paaca Nova's traditional socio-economic structures, along with their independence. With the Indian threat removed, rubber tappers began to enter the area. After the discovery of cassiterite on the upper reaches of the rivers, prospectors poured into the region and cut off all possibilities of retreat. The Indians had no option but to increasingly participate in an alien social and economic world. Immediately after pacification they were in no position to oppose relocation and congregation, the loss of many kinsmen through disease had so traumatized survivors that they were unable to put up much resistance, and the epidemics had so reduced their numbers that many groups were unable to continue as independent units. Some merger was necessary. Many of the Pacaa Nova in this period also feared renewed attacks by rubber gatherers, which was precisely why the Oro mbun came out with José Dias at Riberão.

But the desire to obtain steel tools and other manufactured goods controlled by the civilizados was ultimately the most important stimulus to resettlement and permanent contact. Steel knives and axes not only played a vital role in the process of attraction and pacification, but also served as key elements for changes in various aspects of culture. Because these tools are so obviously superior to stone and wood to horticultural peoples, tribes can develop a "thirst for iron" (Schaden 1969:179). Much of the Indian raiding had as its objective the acquisition of iron tools (Nordenskiold 1922:117). Their desire for the metal was so great that the Tupari consciously braved the inevitable epidemics to obtain it. Caspar (1956:145) writes: "One of the main reasons why Indians who in the last two hundred years have had negative experiences with whites finally agree to make peace is their demand for iron tools, especially machetes, knives and axes." (author's translation.)

As late as 1970, iron tools were still the most prized trade items. Families had at least one or two machetes, several knives and, occasionally, an axe or a pair of scissors. Fish-hooks and nylon line became important at the new settlements, where fish became the major protein source. During my stay, I exchanged over five hundred fish-hooks and thousands of meters of nylon fishing line as well as the ever-popular knives and machetes.

Once the appetite for iron took hold, the Pacaa Nova were forced to maintain a permanent relationship in order to satisfy it. It also compelled them to give something in exchange, and this necessitated entry into the regional extractive economy or dependence on a mission or the Indian Agency.

The Indian Agency post initially encouraged the Pacaa Nova to cut rubber; between 1962 and 1964 as many as one hundred of them worked in the rubber forests at the headwaters of the Rio Pacaas Novas and the Rio Nova. Others, at Posto Dr. Tanajura and the nearby settlement of Pitop, earned cash by producing a surplus of manioc flour to be sold in Guajará Mirim. At Sagarana, trade goods were obtained through a type of wage labor. In each of these situations, the Pacaa Nova were drawn into an alien system over which they had no control. Economic activities began to reflect the interests of nuclear families, and weakened the system of reciprocal exchanges that had linked larger social units through a network of mutual obligations. The use of steel tools facilitated and encouraged greater individual initiative: it became more common to see individuals preparing large gardens or building their own houses. These economic changes impeded the processes of recovery from the epidemics and attempts to rebuild a functioning community in the new settlements, weakening the Pacaa Nova's resistance to outsiders.

Shotguns had a similar effect, but created a more immediate dependence because they required a steady supply of shells, lead, powder and firing caps. Most of the men at Pitop, Dr. Tanajura, the Lage and Rio Negro had guns, whereas those at Sagarana had only recently obtained a few. Guns are becoming integrated into Pacaa Nova hunting practices and are now indispensable to the younger men most of whom are unwilling and perhaps unable to hunt with bow and arrow. Like iron tools, guns decrease the emphasis on group activity. Where, formerly, several hunters cooperated in a tapir or pig hunt, now a hunter can go out alone with expectations of success and without the prospect of having to track wounded prey over long distances. Security legislation passed in 1972 to license owners of guns and control the purchase of ammunition has made it more difficult to obtain weapons, especially for Indians, who are generally not registered with the police. The new legislation favours those associated with the missions or the Indian Services and strengthens the control exercised by these institutions.

The special significance and importance of steel and guns for Amazonian tribes is symbolized by their rapid incorporation into various creation myths. (Schaden 1969:190).

Relocation along navigable rivers and in areas populated by rubber tappers or frequently visited by traders, missionaries and government officials has made clothing indispensable. Among rural Brazilians, clothing is an essential aspect of "humanness"; it separates people from animals. In the past, the appearance of naked Indians inevitably triggered a violent response. In self-defence, the Pacaa Nova quickly covered up. But clothing also indicates a change of status from *Indio*

Bravo (or wild Indian) to a more civilized *Indio Manso* (tame Indian) or *Caboclo*. (Snethlage 1937:126).

Attractive clothing has become highly desirable, with the demand for it, almost as great as that for iron tools. Attempts by the Indian Service to unload poor-quality, ill-fitting clothing met with resistance and complaints. The Pacaa Nova who worked for the Catholic missionary in Guajará Mirim and had the opportunity to purchase their own clothing were often better-dressed than lower class urban Brazilians. In the evangelical missions, demand for clothing became so great that the missionaries introduced treadle sewing machines and gave the women sewing lessons.

Sewing machine introduced by missionaries at Pitop.

I also noticed that a wide variety of manufactured products — hammocks, mosquito nets, tin cans, aluminum pots, scissors, soap, toothbrushes, flashlights and even the occasional radio or suitcase — had made their way into Indian homes. Items such as toothpaste were traded and used for the exclusive purpose of appearing more like the

Brazilians, with the expectation of impressing the local civilizado population as well as the missionaries or Indian agents.

Patterns of trade, and especially awareness of the value of manufactured items, varied with geographic location. Knowledge of market prices was directly proportional to distance from Brazilian population centres or to ease of access to such centres. In Lage, Pitop and Posto Dr. Tanajura most exchange was conducted through the Indian Service or the missionaries, both of whom brought individuals or groups into town with their produce and helped them to negotiate prices. With this help, the Oro nao and Oro waram were able to bargain more effectively and buy manufactured goods at lower cost. I bargained with the Oro nao at Tanajura, and found them much more adept and more knowledgeable about relative values than those at Sagarana. At the more distant posts, such as Riberão and Rio Negro, Indians rarely visited the city, content to let missionaries or the Indian Service act as intermediaries. Sagarana was a special case: control was much more concentrated in the hands of the administration, in a system that will later be discussed in detail.

Wage labour was relatively rare, but some Pacaa Nova from Tanajura and Rio Negro continued to work as hunters, guides, and general helpers at the rubber camps. A number of young men from Sagarana were employed at Prelacy enterprises in Guajará Mirim. They were housed and fed at the medical centre and received a small salary. Although their daily lives and freedom of movement were strictly regulated, they were better fed and were able to acquire more manufactured items than Pacaa Nova at the mission. Young, unmarried men at Sagarana showed a keen interest in going to Guajará Mirim in order to acquire such prized items as shotguns or radios.

The epidemics had orphaned a large number of adolescent females on the Rio Negro. This meant that men who married them would be able to avoid bride service. In the early sixties, men from Pitop and Tanajura went to the Rio Negro to bring back wives, creating a precedent for marriage into a group with whom one did not have kin relations, and perhaps accounting for the strong trend to virilocality that Mason found at Pitop and Tanajura. In communities like Sagarana, made up of remnants of all named groups, the majority of new marriages were with members of other groups. Expectations related to the pattern of past exchanges were frequently frustrated and led to ill feeling. A number of marriages violated the incest taboo, but occurred because of the exigencies of the new situation or the possibility of appealing to outside mediation. In one case, a marriage between parallel cousins was supported by the Catholic missionary, although the couple were criticised by their kin.

Responsibility over much of the Indian population was divided between Catholics and Protestant evangelicals who discouraged intermarriage, which increased the difficulty of finding marriage partners. Sagarana had a shortage of marriageable females, while Pitop and Tanajura had a surplus, which created self-evident problems and was used to try to lure men out of the Catholic mission.

Relocation obviously spelled the end of independent decision-making, but also affected the exercise of influence within the settlement. The traditional skills of leaders were no longer sufficient. New skills, such as knowledge of Portuguese and the ability to interact successfully with outsiders or to negotiate exchanges, became equally important. In the evangelical missions, once conversion had occurred, the ability to read the translated sections of the Bible became a prerequisite of leadership.

Dependence meant that the arena of political decision making was now dominated by members of another ethnic group, whose control rested on their ability to manipulate the Indians through a combination of force, control over trade goods and medicines, and control over operational information. They were also able to exploit the inability of the wari to solve inter-group problems in the relocated villages. The degree of dependence and dominance will be illustrated in a later discussion of the mission post of Sagarana.

Traditional ritual observances rapidly disappeared, or were carried out in greatly attenuated form. The missionaries and Indian agents were horrified at the wari's elaborate mortuary rituals and rites associated with killing and caused these practices to disappear almost immediately. The Pacaa Nova now refuse to talk about them; the only glimpses we have are through brief comments in the unpublished material collected by New Tribes Missions. To what degree they were practiced in secret in the woods in the early years is difficult to determine; data from both the Protestant mission and from Sagarana indicate that they were practiced for some time.

Elaborate community rituals like the chicha feast were initially suspended because of the shortage of maize in the years following pacification. They were revived in 1964 at Posto Dr. Tanajura and Dois Irmãos, only to be suspended in 1968 when the evangelicals managed to convert members of these posts. The two feasts that I witnessed at Sagarana in 1970 were devoid of much of the ritual elaboration and symbolic interaction that was described in the 1964 ceremony. The ritual paraphernalia used in the celebration, especially the drums and the flutes, were sloppily made at the last minute, in direct contrast to the care that was formerly taken in the manufacture of these items. Some of the instruments and costumes of the earlier feast were entirely absent in 1970. The drums, formerly made of ceramic, were replaced by tin cans covered with strips of sun-dried rubber. Nevertheless, time was still spent in clearing a path from the forest, and the invited group still appeared painted with black dye or genipapa and with hair bedecked with eagle down. Women participated very little in the ceremony with the exception of one unmarried, adolescent girl among the visitors, who also drank chicha. The circumstances at Sagarana made more elaborate preparations difficult and, in the new social context, the maintenance of inter-group ties were perceived as less relevant than before.

Other, less dramatic ceremonies, like wailing over game or the communal singing at the time of the new moon, were no longer practiced when outsiders were present. At some posts, new economic activities such as rubber gathering conflicted with the traditional ceremonial cycle, and ritual declined in proportion to increasing participation in the outside economy.

The wari view of the spiritual universe is more resistant to change. Despite the abandonment of many of the communal rituals, the traditions continue to be passed on. They still sing and dance — and children aged six or seven already have an impressive repertoire — the spirits still influence behavior, and food taboos continue to regulate the diet. "Converted," evangelical Indians might ignore certain prohibitions when visiting the town, but back in the village the power of spirit entities remains unchallenged, much to the chagrin of the missionaries.

The first conversions to evangelical Protestantism took place in 1968. New Tribes missionaries had worked in the area since 1954; their efforts and persistence were rewarded when three Oro nao from Dois Irmãos consented to baptism. Since then, the movement has spread to include most of the Indians at Posto Dr. Tanajura and the neighbouring villages of Pitop, Posto Tenente Lira and Rio Negro-Ocaia. The New Tribes Mission has published several booklets in the Pacaa Nova language, among them a translation of a section of the Bible. Acceptance of Protestantism involved the rejection of drinking, and since the conversions there have been no chicha feasts in their missions. Converts have abandoned traditional songs (all of which, the missionaries claimed, had sexual connotations) and have replaced them with translated Christian hymns. Chicha feasts and club fights, or at least the functions of these, have been replaced by weekly cult meetings at which grievances are presented and discussed, and often solved by the missionaries who function as mediators. The weekly meeting provides a new social focus, as well as a means of attaining prestige and influence for the younger, more acculturated members of the community who have mastered the difficult task of reading passages of the Bible. With the backing of the influential missionaries, they dominate these meetings, thereby playing an important role in group decision-making. The missionaries have tried to select such leaders from the dominant kin groups in the village.

The acceptance of Protestantism is related to the entire complex of socio-economic changes, i.e. the weakening of traditional society. The old beliefs no longer served to explain the world just as the traditional curers were no longer able to cope with the diseases introduced by Europeans. In contrast to the largely negative interactions with the dominant Brazilian world, relations with members of the New Tribes Mission were friendly; the missionaries dealt with them fairly, did not molest their women, and were always there to help. In their campaign to convert the Indians, they promoted the idea that all human beings are equal before Christ. When converts from the Rio Negro visited Sagarana they expressed this concept of equality with the message that "all men (sic) have the blood of Christ." The emphasis on this aspect of the message highlights the Indians' desire to feel equal to members of the dominant society and to overcome the inferior position imposed on them by members of that society.

The influence of the missionaries is clearly attributable to their long-term commitment to the Pacaa Nova and, more importantly, to the fact that they are the only outsiders who speak the Indian language and have some knowledge of native culture. They have been able to act as brokers between the wari and outsiders, especially the Indian Service and business houses in Guajará Mirim. Frequently, it is the female member of the New Tribes Mission family who devotes herself to the linguistic aspect of the work. As a result of her familiarity with the language and culture, she often plays a more important role in decision-making and the solution of conflicts at the mission. She may be more highly regarded and more influential than her husband and, on occasion, may serve as a role model for the indigenous women.

Sagarana:
A Case Study of Dependence

The debacle of pacification and the sensational publicity that followed, generated mutual recriminations between Catholics and Indian Service bureaucracy. To hide its own dubious role, the Service shifted most of the blame onto the Prelacy and banned Catholic mission activity among the Pacaa Nova. The evangelicals, who had refrained from criticism, were banned only briefly and so had the field to themselves for a few years.

Meanwhile, the bishop requested the help of his French-based order in locating a doctor who could deal with the serious lack of medical care for the Prelacy's rural population and for the newly contacted Pacaa Nova. In 1963, the Order sent a doctor-priest, (Padre medico), along with a large quantity of medical supplies.

While access to the Pacaa Nova was forbidden, the Padre devoted himself to the assistance of other indigenous groups. He acquired a reputation on the frontier for helping to combat measles epidemics among the Xavante and, later, the Bororo of Mato Grosso. In 1964, he was instrumental in dealing with an outbreak of cholera in Beni province, Bolivia. With financial contributions from Catholic charities in Europe, he turned a large riverboat into a floating hospital and initiated regular medical services to the more remote areas of the Prelacy, which had never seen a doctor before.

Among the newly contacted Pacaa Nova, the danger of outbreaks of disease had not yet passed. In 1964, an epidemic of measles broke out at SPI post Major Amarante at Riberão. The agent there was unprepared, as usual, to deal with a large-scale outbreak; lacking antibiotics or medical training, he was forced to turn to the Prelacy for assistance. A relief expedition led by the new Padre quickly brought the situation under control. In recognition of this help, the Catholics were again granted access to the Pacaa Nova.

This turn of events led the Prelacy to negiotiate the establishment of a mission. Initial attempts to secure the area of Riberão, the most northerly and the oldest of the Indian Service posts, proved unsuccessful, although a number of Indian Service agents and employees supported it. Negotiations then began over land at the junction of the Mamoré and Guaporé rivers on the Bolivian border, including the area referred to lo-

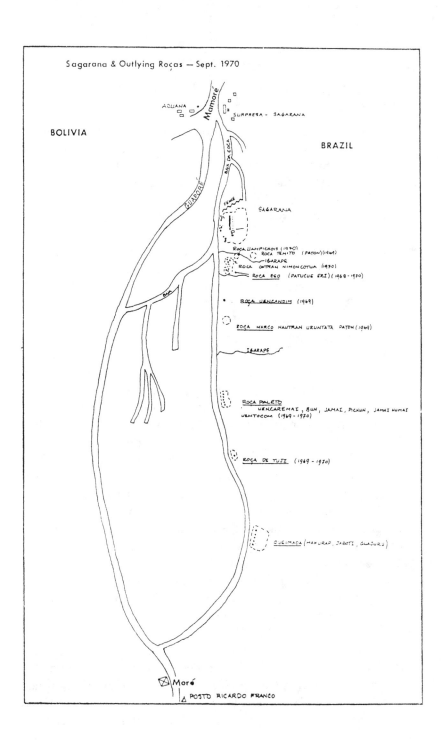

Sagarana & Outlying Roças — Sept. 1970

BOLIVIA

BRAZIL

ADUANA

SURPRESA - SAGARANA

SAGARANA

Roça UAMPICHOIS (1970)
Roça TEMITO (PATON)(1969)
IGARAPE
Roça ONTRAN NIMON COTUA (1970)
Roça ESO (PATUCUE ERI)(1968-1970)

ROÇA UENCANDIM (1969)

ROÇA MARCO NAUTRAN URUNTATA PATON (1969)

IGARAPE

ROÇA PALETO
UENCAREMAI, BUN, JAMAI, PICHUN, JAMAI HUMAI
UENTOCOM (1969-1970)

ROÇA DE TUJI (1969-1970)

QUEIMADA (MAKURAP, JABOTI, GUAJURU)

Moré

POSTO RICARDO FRANCO

cally as the *boca* (mouth) of the Guaporé. Although suitable for agriculture the area was outside traditional tribal territory, and involved a long journey along the Mamoré.

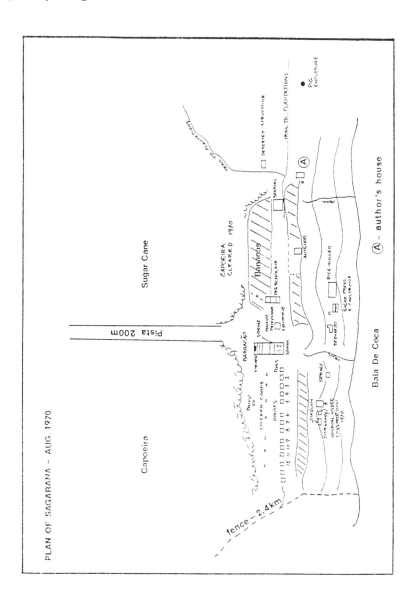

PLAN OF SAGARANA – AUG. 1970

The land included the civilizado settlement of Surprêsa and much of the area to the south. It had been cleared and settled in the 1930s by a colonist from the Brazilian northeast, who brought with him a labour force of sixteen families, mostly Bolivian Indians and mestizos, people of mixed race. Despite attacks by the Moré and Itén, he had succeeded in establishing a prosperous plantation, with large tracts of coffee and sugar cane. His heirs showed little interest in continuing the plantation and business, and left it unattended until the 1950s, when an agricultural school and an orphanage were established on the plantation grounds. The school failed, and the site was abandoned in 1959.

Women making maize beer at Sagarana.

In 1965, the Prelacy of Guajará Mirim was granted the concession to Surprêsa and to a stretch of land twenty-eight kilometers along the Guaporé to the border of the SPI post of Ricardo Franco. The concession gave the Prelacy ownership and control on condition that a settlement be built for the recently pacified Pacaa Nova and that educational and health services be provided for the region.

The area of Surprêsa lies between the two major rubber zones of the Madeira and Mato Grosso. As was earlier noted, both areas suffered severe decreases in population and were partly abandoned after the collapse of the rubber boom. In the 1920s and 1930s, some of the land around Surprêsa was converted to agricutural use. Despite attacks by the Moré, a number of plantations and ranches were established on both sides of the Guaporé, stretching south toward Principe da Beira (Snethlage 1937:15). The region as a whole was sparsely populated, particularly the areas away from the main rivers, along the branches or *baias*. The latter are old ox-bows, which still abound in wildlife. However, within the last decade, fish and turtles, the most important protein sources, have declined rapidly in numbers because of commercial overfishing.

The Brazilian and Bolivian population of the area, mostly descendants of the earlier settlers, were largely subsistence agriculturalists practising shifting cultivation. In 1968, there were more than fifty families within a short distance of the boca. Their "fields," rarely exceeding two or three hectares and contained beans, manioc and bananas. Most families kept domesticated animals, notably chickens, ducks and pigs, and did some hunting and fishing. Some lemons, limes, oranges and pineapples were cultivated for sale to Guajará Mirim or to passing boats, and, at the end of the dry season, a few local men participated in commercial fishing. Alligator, wild pig, cats and jaguars were hunted for their hides. The cash earned through these activities paid for outside goods. Most business transactions were conducted with passing river boats or with small trading enterprises that cruised the rivers with floating stores *(regatões)*. Regular communication with Guajará Mirim was facilitated by motor vessels that plied the Mamoré and Guaporé, transporting fish, agricultural produce, cattle, rubber, Brazil nuts and hides. A regular monthly service by the Serviço de Navegação de Guaporé linked Guajará Mirim and Vila Bela, the former capital of the captaincy of Mato Grosso.

On the Bolivian side of the border, the government maintained a customs post to guard against the passage of contraband up the Mamoré river. On occasion, it functioned as a base for soldiers sent to keep out Brazilian fishermen.

The closest Indian settlement was the Indian Service Post Ricardo Franco, which lay approximately two hours to the south by motor boat. In 1970, it housed half a dozen families, remnants of various tribal groups (Canoé, Parintintin, Jaboti, and Makuráp) who had been in contact since the 1920s and 1930s. Most of their kin had left the area in the 1950s and

1960s, but the post continued to function because the Service invested in a small herd of cattle. When I visited in 1967, the administration of the post was in shambles; the agent was in Guajará Mirim and the remaining native families were dissatisfied and eager to move out. As the Prelacy had obtained the area of Surprêsa, some officials of the Indian Service suggested that the padres should take over Posto Ricardo Franco as well.

The other official Indian settlement in the area was the Nucleo Indigenal Moré, on the Bolivian side of the Guaporé, a few miles north of Ricardo Franco. The Nucleo was established in 1937 as part of a government project of "Indigenous Schools" aimed at sedentarising the Moré and Itén. It had a more paternalistic, authoritarian administration than Ricardo Franco; life there was strictly regimented by civilizado administrators and a "patron." The Moré were primarily subsistence farmers, but also sold some surplus produce or hired themselves out as unskilled labour to neighbouring ranches. Recently, they have begun to produce highly decorative native crafts, and have been moderately successful in marketing them to passing river boats and to a few buyers from Guajará Mirim who come to the Moré specifically for that purpose.

The Project

The Prelacy, already engaged in pastoral work in the community of Principe de Beira to the south, decided to focus its project at the boca on the economic development of the region as a whole. Surprêsa was to be the nucleus of an agricultural colony and regional cooperative — the Colonia Agricola Sagarana — that would involve the independent non-Indian farmers along the Guaporé and Mamoré rivers. The padres planned to provide medical assistance, a school, advice on cash crops, marketing and storage, and to organize regular transportation of produce to Guajará Mirim. In the late sixties, the Prelacy had built a large barracão that served as a school and storage facility, and was in the process of building a large motor vessel to transport local produce to market and bring various social services to the local inhabitants. Future plans included the construction of a sugar refinery, for which a licence, the first to be granted in Rondônia, had already been obtained.

At the time of this study (1969/70), development of the broader program had been hindered by lack of interest and initiative, caused by what the priests refer to as the "paternalistic expectations" of the local inhabitants. Attempts to encourage self-motivation had failed, and the

Prelacy was unable, and unwilling, to take on the role of the traditional "patron".

Although the Pacaa Nova mission, officially named "Vila Coronel Tosta," was seen as an integral part of a larger project, it was to be physically and administratively separate. Its official designation was rarely used and in the rest of this account I will continue to refer to the Indian settlement as Sagarana.

In the fall of 1965, land was cleared for the mission settlement on an ox-bow about five miles from the confluence of the Mamoré and Guaporé. The site itself, judging by the quantity and variety of ceramic shards, had been previously inhabited by different Amerindian groups.

The School at Sagarana.

In November, work started on a large central building — a combination school, kitchen, storage shed and meeting place. Employees of the Prelacy supervised the carpentry and hired local labour to assist a workforce of Indian men from Riberão. In the first year, these Indians were the mission's only inhabitants. They were lodged in a series of mission-built huts extending in a line along the top of an escarpment overlooking the water.

In early 1966, the Prelacy appointed the Padre as director of the project. His excellent reputation as a frontier doctor, his wide-ranging political contacts, and especially his track record as a fundraiser made him the obvious choice for the position. In turn, the directorship of a mission of recently pacified natives translated into added prestige for him, since the "Indian problem" had become a *cause celebre* in urban circles in Brazil and abroad. As head of a mission for the "savage, cannibalistic" Pacaa Nova, who had terrorized Rondônia for the last decade, the Padre was sought out by virtually every important visitor who came to Guajará Mirim. During my initial three-month stay in the area, I met the regional governor, high-ranking military officers, and "wealthy friends" of Catholic charity organizations at his house.

Preparations for Research

My first visit to Sagarana in 1967 was as a guest of the Padre. In the Padre's sleek speedboat, we covered the distance to the mission in a mere five hours, despite the ever-present danger of semi-submerged logs and sandbars. As we reached the confluence of the Guaporé and Mamoré, and the site of Surprêsa, we entered a spur of the river, and within a short time came upon a clearing. There, on a hill, stood a row of neatly spaced huts with a very large building at one end. The roar of the powerful Rolls Royce inboard engine had announced our arrival, and a tight knot of people stood at the dock as we slid into shore. A young, stocky man, with a six-shooter strapped to his belt, stepped forward to make the boat fast, and then greeted the Padre with a heartfelt *abraço* (bearhug). An equally sincere but somewhat more reserved welcome was extended by a second, much older man with deepset yellow eyes. I was surprised to discover that the first, a man barely in his twenties, was the overseer — the man in charge of the mission. The other, Bernardo, had arrived the previous year to set up a school, which was housed in the large building above. His deepset yellow eyes were the legacy of an almost fatal snake bite earlier that year. For the next two days, these two men were my guides as we toured the fields and facilities of the mission.

Two years later, Bernardo was my host, as I made the necessary preparations for a more lengthy stay.

Sagarana 1970

When I returned in 1970, a small house had been prepared for me on the outskirts of the village. The mission itself had become much larger, and its organization more complex, which made it easier for me to gain some independence from the mission administration.

As I walked toward the school one morning, I noticed a dugout from the boca tying up at the dock below. I recognized its occupant as Antonio, the brother-in-law of Joaquim who ran the mission dispensary. He and his family had moved to the boca shortly after Joaquim's arrival, and had become a frequent visitor at Sagarana. I knew that he had

The settlement of Sagarana.

recently returned from Guajará Mirim. In the hope that he had some letters for me, I made my way down to the dispensary. Five younger women with small children were patiently waiting on the veranda for their aspirins or cough syrups. Inside, the two men were drinking a *cafezinho*, the strong sweet coffee so popular with Brazilians. Antonio had no mail for me, but he said that the Padre was preparing his floating hospital and would be arriving within a week to visit Sagarana, the Nucleo Indigenal Moré, and the Indian Service post of Ricardo Franco. In the past, these trips had been more frequent, but other interests and concerns were now taking up the Padre's time. The news restored my good spirits, not only because of the possibility of mail from home, but also because of the opportunity it provided me to observe the Padre's role in the mission and his interactions with his employees and with the Pacaa Nova. I was beginning to feel that such information would help me considerably in understanding Sagarana. My work was progressing all too slowly and my self-confidence was at an all-time low.

The Overseer

On my way to the outlying gardens, I ran into the overseer and gave him Antonio's message. His relief was evident. Fresh supplies were sorely needed: it had been difficult for him in the past three or four weeks, to recruit Indian labour without trade goods. In the old days, trade goods had been stocked at the mission, and the "store" was opened every Sunday morning, when the local in-house currency could be redeemed for knives, fishhooks, cloth, soap, shotgun shells, hammocks, mosquito nets, and a host of other items. These Sunday mornings had been a festive and exciting occasion for the Indians. There was great demand for these goods, and the overseer made the best of it. He praised those who were the most diligent, and lectured others on the merits of honest labour and the rewards that it brought in material goods, as well as the added benefit of the Padre's approval. In those days, there was no shortage of men who would work six days a week to earn a one-day bonus. Men like Paton and Uencaremai had worked steadily for five months to accumulate sufficient money for a shotgun, but recently only Pauiam had shown similar dedication. Some of the Indians had turned to the boca, and others were trading with the nearby settlement of Makuráp and Jabotí, which in turn dealt with passing traders.

The overseer often reminisced about the early years of the mission, when his word was law and the Indians were more disciplined and more pliable. He had taken seriously his task of civilizing the Indian — teaching them to work and bringing them into the twentieth century — and he was proud of the fact that the Padre had placed so much trust in him despite his youth. He was determined to repay this trust with total loyalty, but the arrival of first Bernardo and then Joaquim had made his life more difficult. They had interfered and sown the seeds of distrust with the Padre; when they weren't complaining about him to the Padre, they were filling the bishop's ear with lies. He sometimes had the impression that they were out to sabotage the entire project. He fought back, but the damage had been done. The trade goods were withdrawn, and with them went the incentive to work, an important factor if he was to achieve his objective.

The younger men had always been the more manageable. They grew up during the hell of the epidemics, but had spent most of their lives in contact with Brazilians. About half of them had worked in Guajará Mirim for one or two years, and several had been in the rubber camps or with the American missionaries and had worked for, and been supervised by, Brazilians. In Sagarana, they lived together and were readily assembled for work in the fields or around the settlement. But even they were now avoiding him. It was time that their enthusiasm be rekindled. Perhaps the Padre could again be persuaded of the necessity of direct rewards for labour. The older men were already lost to him. The moment the Prelacy had allowed them to move out of the settlement (over his strenuous objections), they could no longer be relied upon to appear regularly for work in the fields. He had known that this would happen, and in the last few years had been pushing the Padre to bring in some of the civilizados from the boca to supervise Indian labour and to provide an example of civilized life, but his arguments had been in vain.

The Padre has listened to Padre Roberto, who had some kind of romantic notion that the Pacaa Nova would voluntarily, or with persuasion, work to produce a surplus that could be sold by the mission. Last year the entire surplus had been consumed, in the form of chicha, at two huge drinking feasts, and preparations were already under way for a repetition. While the Paaca Nova all lived at the mission, the overseer had been able to put an end to these excesses, and it had been possible to have the mission in good order for the Padre's visits, but last year, a disgustingly drunken scene was played out in front of a visiting

French priest. The Padre, who had wanted to show the visitor how well the Pacaa Nova were progressing and how successfully they were integrating into Brazilian frontier society, had been furious. He liked to have a little native flavour, perhaps some singing or dancing when he brought visitors, especially potential donors, to the mission. But how could he ask for a threshing machine for a people who could exhibit such disgraceful behaviour?

The overseer had warned the Padre that allowing the Paaca Nova to practice their own culture might lead to incidents of this sort. In the early years, before his marriage, he had devoted all his time and energy to civilizing these savages. He had been vigilant night and day, had bribed the younger men to keep him informed of goings on in the mission and, on occasion, had even risked his life to impose civilized standards of behaviour, but all this had been undone by the new policy of decentralization.

The change, however, suited his wife, who had never liked his living with savages. At least now he spent more time at home, and even accompanied her when she wanted to visit her family across the river from Surprêsa. Her father often remarked that Brazilians had never really known how to deal with these savages. In Bolivia they knew how to use the whip, but in Brazil, he had heard that a seringalista had been arrested by the SPI on a complaint for raising a whip to one of his Indian rubber tappers.

The overseer was preoccupied with these thoughts as he made his way to his house to tell his wife the news. Much work would have to be done to prepare Sagarana for the visit. The Padre would bring cooking oil and flour, donated by the Americans through the Alliance for Progress, and he could look forward to receiving some maize, sweet potatoes, dried fish, and salted meat to take back with him. The next few days would have to be spent in search of *tambaki*, a large fish that could only be found in the vicinity of certain trees whose ripe seeds, falling to the water, provided its favorite food; or in trolling for *traira*, a fish found during this time of the year in the deeper channels of the river. If they were lucky, they might even encounter a few troops of howler monkeys on the way. The overseer called Pauiam and told him to inform Bernardo of the news and then to get some of the bachelors together for a clean-up. The news of the upcoming visit had already circulated through the settlement. José, who had been building a shelf for Joaquim's kitchen, had overhead Antonio's announcement, as had the women waiting on the veranda. Word spread quickly; José ran to tell his wife to inform her father, who had been working on a few arrows to trade with the Padre, but had been unable to finish them because no macaw feathers had been available for the colourful fringe above the flight feathers. Paleto, whose wife had been at the dispensary with their year-old son, was already on his way to tell his kin the news.

The next week would be one of feverish activity, as everyone at the mission and those in the surrounding gardens hastily harvested crops of beans, maize, or sweet potatoes, rounded up their chickens, turned to the production of drums and flutes, or made copies of the colourful headdresses they had seen the Padre bring from the Moré.

Uamchai

José, or Uamchai as he was known among his fellow wari, was looking forward to a new shirt and the bright red dress that he would buy for his new wife. For the past two months, he had worked six days a week at the mission and had received the full weekly salary, which included a day's bonus. Like some of the other younger men, he had spent over a year in Guajará Mirim and had learned the use of a saw and hammer. That skill, and his relative fluency in Portuguese, had definitely been an advantage in Sagarana. He knew how to deal with civilizados or wijam and was successful in obtaining the goods his family wanted.

But contact with them had not always been like this. He remembered the days when wijam had not been as stingy and had provided them with gifts of knives and cloth. But those days had also been a period of sadness. When the strangers first came, sickness had swept the land, and all those of importance to him had died. His mother's brother, burning up with fever, had plunged into the river and had died on its bank. For months the staccato of the deathwail was heard everywhere. There was no food, since no one was capable of hunting, or even of harvesting the manioc and maize that grew in the gardens.

He had gone to join other Oro eo, who had concentrated around the wijam at their village on the Rio Negro. There, surrounded by Oro at and Oro nao, many of them strangers, he had felt ill at ease. When the wijam, known as Padre, came to the post to look after the sick and to recruit wari with promises of gifts, he and his cousin had gone with him. On their trip downriver, several boys his own age from the Oro nao villages joined them. Eager for adventure, and with no relatives to go back to, Uamchai was quite content in Guajará Mirim in the company of other young wari.

Oro mbun — one of group contacted in 1969.

Occasionally, distant relatives came to the city in the company of white men (evangelical missionaries) who spoke the dialect of the Oro nao and tried to persuade him to come to their village, where he would be in the company of some of his kin and where he might find a wife. He had refused their overtures. Life at the Padre's large compound had been exciting and food and trade goods plentiful. On weekends, Padre would load them into the Prelacy truck and take them to the nearby forest to hunt with shotguns. If he was to leave, he must have a shotgun first, and he would have to work in the Padre's brick factory a little longer. Although he felt uncomfortable among most wijam, he had come to trust and even like some of the black men who worked with him in the brick factory. In town, he was treated with more respect than the Oro nao who came with the *crente* (evangelicals), since he was under the protection of Padre, who was a powerful healer among the wijam.

José's life had changed with the arrival in Guajará Mirim of Uem-tocom, an Oro nao from the Rio Novo who had been working with his family in the seringal. Uemtocom had already lost two of his children to the terrible fever, and had brought his family to the Padre in order to save the life of his youngest son. But it was too late; the child was already too weak. With Uemtocom came two older offspring, a son who would soon be a man, and an attractive daughter of marriageable age. Aware of the competition, José lost no time in courting her, and asked her father to accept him as a son-in-law. When Uemtocom decided to resettle in Sagarana, José accompanied him. The older man, used to living independently, ran afoul of the overseer and, rather than tolerating his authoritarianism, decided to remove himself and his family to the gardens farthest from the centre. He also warned his family not to have anything to do with civilizados. José, who enjoyed going to the boca and occasionally played soccer there, quarrelled with his father-in-law over this. On one occasion, when his new wife wanted to leave a celebration at the house of one of the mission employees, he decided to stay and sent her home on her own. Uemtocom was enraged by his behaviour; "talk" quickly escalated into a challenge for a club fight. Several cousins took José's side and Uemtocom got the worst of it. However, the flow of blood on both sides cooled them off, and José returned to live with his wife and her father. He began to spend more time at the gardens and, with his cousin, planted a crop of beans to sell to Padre.

He still continued to work at the centre, but not exclusively for the overseer. His skills were also in demand by Bernardo and Joaquim, and lately by the two young women who ran the kindergarten. He had used his access to other civilizados to get away from the demands of the overseer, and, if his calculations were correct, the two women were more influential with the Padre than either Bernardo or Joaquim. They had shown astonishment when he recited some of the stories he had heard about the overseer, stories gleaned from the Oro mbun and the Oro waramciyey, who had been at the post from the beginning. Talk was, after all, the major tactic in influencing people's behavior. It had not checked the overseer's behavior in the past, but he felt that the two women might succeed in doing so.

Life at the gardens among his fellow Oro eo, Oro at, and Oro nao was good. Unlike the mission post, where constant interference and ridicule from the overseer and the other civilizados made life uncomfortable, the gardens brought back memories of his childhood. The talk of the men coming back from the hunt, reliving their encounters in the forest with game and sometimes with spirits, evoked a nostalgia in him. Paleto, the oldest and most knowledgeable among them, often spoke of the time before the entry of wijam, when game and fish were more plentiful and when many people came together to drink and socialize. There had been many Oro nao and Oro eo, and in those days, people were happy. They sang and danced at the time of the full moon, often staying up all night.

Singing and dancing had returned at the gardens and the wari again made chicha, but it was not like the days when people lived in different parts of the country and would congregate several times a year in larger groups. Paleto, the acknowledged leader of the group, had encouraged the making of chicha the previous year, and after months of preparation had invited the Oro waramciyey and the Oro mbun to drink at his home. He had again painted himself with jaguar spots in honour of his guardian spirit. The visitors drank much chicha and acquitted themselves well; three of them had "died." Three months later the Oro waramciyey had invited the Oro nao to drink at the mission, but only Aitcatchim had died. At the mission, in the presence of the wijam, much of the excitement and pleasure, as well as the elaborate preparations, had disappeared. For weeks, the overseer spoke disparagingly of the occasion, making the younger men feel ashamed.

Early Mission History

Together with Padre Roberto, who had been involved with the pacification effort, the Padre Medico visited the settlement on a monthly basis in late 1965, to bring additional settlers and supplies and to provide medical attention for Indians, local Brazilians and Bolivians. The two priests supervised the early construction but made no attempt to indoctrinate the Indians.

By April 1966, the indigenous population had reached sixty. This was a period of rapid adjustment for the Pacaa Nova. Different remnant groups were being thrown together; they found the new living arrangement difficult. Conflicts were frequent and resulted in constant movement in and out of the mission. One group of twenty, from the Rio Lage, stayed only a few days and then left for Ricardo Franco. From there they were returned to Posto Tenente Lira by the Indian Service. Another smaller group returned overland to the headwaters of the Rio Pacaas Novas, a lengthy and arduous journey. Others lived in the nearby bush for periods of two to six months but ultimately returned, drawn by sickness or by a need to replenish supplies of axes and knives.

During his regular medical visits to Indian Service posts the Padre actively recruited settlers for his new mission. Sagarana grew rapidly.

Many of the newcomers were orphans or individuals who did not have close relatives. Many of them were young males, which created an imbalance between males and females in the fifteen to twenty-five year age group at Sagarana.

By June 1967, the settlement had grown to ninety-seven, including a group of Makuráp and Jabotí from the rubber estates of the Rio Branco, a tributary of the Guaporé, who were brought to Sagarana by the Indian Service. After a short stay at the main settlement, they chose to move to a site referred to as the Queimada, on the periphery of mission territory where they were less exposed to outside interference and control.

The Prelacy's original aim was to provide an economic base for the Pacaa Nova and to shelter them from random outside contacts until they were capable and confident enough to run their own affairs and to deal with outsiders. To this end, the Prelacy planned to create a model agricultural enterprise that would familiarize the Indians with new methods of agriculture and the operation of a market economy. Although the settlement was initially structured like a traditional plantation, with Indian labour under civilizado control, the padres envisaged a system where the Pacaa Nova would be motivated to run the settlement on their own with only minimal guidance. A visitor at the post wrote in *Lettre d'Amazonie* (1968:14) that the padres wanted the colony "to orient itself progressively toward a cooperative system" where each would exploit a parcel of land presumably granted in usufruct by the adminstration. The introduction of new crops and new techniques of planting and livestock raising would increase production and diversify the economic base, replacing reliance on hunting and foraging. Only after survival and economic self-sufficiency were ensured would spiritual matters be given consideration.

Although planning and policy were determined by the Padre in Guajará Mirim, direct supervision and control over the daily affairs of the settlement were placed in the hands of a local overseer, in this case a seventeen-year-old Bolivian with no previous experience of native people. He had been employed by the Padre as a driver, and was entrusted with this important position because of his dependability, readiness to learn, ambition, and above all his unquestioning loyalty to the Padre. His tasks were to supervise the construction of the facilities, establish the gardens, maintain order in the mission, and accustom the Indians to a settled existence and orderly life.

The overseer conscientiously set about to do the Padre's work, but he interpreted the intent quite differently. Unlike the director and the padres of the Prelacy, he had been brought up on the frontier and shared its highly discriminatory view of Indians. To him, the native population's obvious inferiority and innate incapacity demanded a firm hand. He was convinced that they were incapable of running their own lives, and used to tell me "They don't know the meaning of honest work... If you leave them to their own devices they will just sit around, pick some fruit when it pleases them, hunt and fish occasionally and generally do as little as possible." This conviction motivated all of his actions and decisions.

The overseer's major objectives were to make the settlement produce, and to civilize the Indians — which to him meant preparing them to work for civilizados. He believed that success could only be achieved through imposition of strict rules and discipline, and through constant watchfulness and intervention to prevent the re-emergence of the "old ways." Traditional subsistence activities — hunting, fishing, or foraging — were not seen as real work. Hunting was deemed recreational, and communal hunts were organized on Sundays in order not to interfere with the work schedule. These limitations kept the hunters close to the village or along the immediate water routes.

During the first part of 1966, he and a Bolivian cook were the only permanent civilizado residents. When necessary, temporary labourers were hired at the boca. They were joined later that year by an agricultural technician, who was contracted to plan the layout of the first fields and to work with the agricultural project at the boca. He remained for eight months to supervise the first planting. The Pacaa Nova were fed by the village kitchen and supplied with manufactured goods in proportion to their participation in an established weekly work schedule.

The discipline and constant supervision in the first few years were reminiscent of the Spanish Jesuit missions of the seventeenth and eighteenth centuries. The following description, taken from Watson (1952:47-48) might almost be a description of the early days in Sagarana:

> Establishing a mission meant that the Indians were obliged to live where the Jesuits indicated, perhaps to join an already organized town. They had quarters assigned to them, were presumably issued "proper clothing" and were allotted work and fields in which it was to be done. The women were often set to weaving cotton like that which characterized the household in-

dustry of Europe of the time. Men apparently did the agricultural work (in probable contrast to the aboriginal pattern). Most of the day's activities were directed by the priests, apparently following a strict schedule, and little was left to the will or inclination of the Indians. Under no circumstances were people to leave reduction without permission. Indians were appointed to various offices, mostly connected with spying, policing and reporting what were henceforth to be considered crimes and misdemeanors. If in one of the barracks, some nostalgic individuals gave themselves over to practicing the old ways, particularly in matters religious, this might be reported. The miscreants would then almost certainly be punished. The punishments, through the political acumen of the fathers, were inflicted by minor officials selected from among the native proselytes themselves.

The inculcation of orderliness and obedience to authority was very noticeable in economic matters. The missions were run as ideally as great agrarian enterprises with peon labour could be - from the point of view of discipline, organization and centralization. Or at least such was the intent.

At Sagarana, as in the Jesuit missions, every hour of the day was organized, from the wake-up bell at 6 a.m. to the time work was to cease. At 7 a.m., men and women assembled at the barracão, where they were issued tools and sent to their various chores. Women assisted in some of the agricultural work, especially planting and weeding, but more frequently were put to work in the kitchen or in maintaining the central clearing. The schedule was rigidly enforced. Meals were served in a communal kitchen and strict rules of dress and cleanliness were imposed. Failure to appear in proper attire (shirts and pants for men, dresses for women) was punished by witholding food rations, a significant inducement to conform since at that time the Indians did not have their own gardens.

The overseer kept detailed records of the number of work days put in by each man and woman. At the end of each week, usually on Saturday evening, the settlement was assembled; amid praise and criticism, the workers were issued old cruzeiro notes in accordance with their labour input, with a bonus for those who worked a full six days. This internal currency, or scrip (in this case, out-of-date banknotes) could only be redeemed at the mission. In the first few years, the scrip could be spent only on Sunday mornings, at which time the overseer opened the stores. After 1967, following a series of misunderstandings between the Padre and the overseer, trade goods were no longer stocked at Sagarana, and the "money" could be used only on the occasion of the Padre's visits. A sample of work records, although from a slightly later period when the situation had changed, indicates that a surprisingly large percentage of the men cooperated in the daily routine. The periods of absence were largely accounted for by illness, usually a mild form of influenza. Despite regular attendance, the output of work was low, since none of the Pacaa Nova had any personal commitment to or say in the tasks they performed.

Little was left "to the inclinations of the Indians," since their inclinations always led them to backslide. To achieve such discipline, the overseer dedicated his every minute to the task. He occupied a house at the end of a row of closely-spaced huts. From this vantage point, he was able to surprise his neighbours and to put an end to singing, drinking, or any kind of social or ritual activity that met with his disapproval, or that might interfere with the Indians' ability to work the next day. He banned communal singing, which usually took place at night at the time of the full moon, and several times threw water on nocturnal gatherings of singers. He tolerated drinking of chicha only on weekends, when the regime of work would not be disrupted. As a consequence of his diligence, the chicha feasts that I witnessed in 1970 had lost much of their original detail, since there was no time for the usual lengthy preparation. He showed little respect for the culture of the wari, of their right to practice their traditions, and applied standards that were not met even by members of his own culture. He ruled Sagarana with a heavy hand, backed by threats of violence. At the time of my first visit to Sagarana, he carried two hand-guns.

His rough and ready notion of justice is illustrated by the case of Tuwo, an Oro nao woman from the Rio Negro who, while living at the house of the Padre in Guajará Mirim, married a parallel cousin who was working in the Padre's compound. Relatives of the two objected strenuously, since the marriage was considered incestuous; but the Padre, unaware of the serious breach of custom, gave them his blessing. Several months after their marriage, they moved to Sagarana. There Tuwo, under pressure from relatives and the community, was persuaded to abort their first child. She was assisted in this by an older relative skilled in such matters. Inevitably, through the network of gossip, it came to the overseer's attention. Incensed by this breach of Christian morality and Brazilian law, he sought out the abortionist, tied her up, and threatened to beat her. At the last moment he changed his mind, probably because her husband was the head of one of the larger kin groups in the village and had a reputation for violence.

Although he did not in this case administer physical punishment, he claimed that he had done so on many other occasions. He attributed his power over the Indians to their fear of him, "since fear is the only thing the caboco [Indian] understands." One afternoon in June, he gave me a dramatic example of his method of "taming" the Indians. While we sat on the porch of his house overlooking the river, two wari were removing a dugout canoe from his dock. Winking at me, he picked his .22 calibre rifle and sent two rounds over their heads. "That will teach them to ask my permission," he said. Startled, the two dove for cover, and for several days the post buzzed with news of the incident and with criticism of the overseer.

Considering his vulnerable position, he acted hastily and often rashly. His real influence, despite his claims, rested on control over medicines and manufactured items, and on insecurity and factionalism of Sargarana's population. He relied heavily on his ability to manipulate these factions and play one off against the other.

He was particularly influential among the younger men who lived in the main barracão, and who, in return for gifts and favours, became his informers. Although there was considerable grumbling and hostility behind his back, and several attempts on his life were plotted, he was able to foil them after being forewarned by his network of informers. Twice, he forestalled such plots and confiscated all weapons in the village. He attributed his survival to his knowledge and understanding of their *jeito* (their way of doing things), as well as to his timely actions.

As is the case with the majority of tribal people in Brazil, the Pacaa Nova were not used to dealing with aggressive behaviour. They could not cope with direct demands. Within their own society, individuals might influence or persuade others to undertake certain courses of action, but could not compel them. Those who overstepped the boundaries of socially accepted behaviour were strongly criticized, subjected to witchcraft, or finally ostracized or killed. Within the mission, these strategies did not work. Retreat from contact was impossible and resistance seemed hopeless. Many of the Indians remembered the punitive expeditions of the 1950s and early 1960s. It seemed easier to tolerate abuses than to face uncertainty, disease and possible violence outside the confines of mission and Indian Service posts.

During the early years, some families and groups of families left the settlement to return to the Indian Service posts in the north; after the initial period, such flights were not easy. Sagarana was about 200 km from the mouth of the Rio Pacaas Novas, and both sides of the Mamoré were settled by civilizados. Most of the runaways were hunted down and returned, some at gunpoint by the overseer, who was either forewarned of their departure or was able to catch them with the mission's motor boat. Once overtaken, they avoided violent confrontation and yielded to the inevitable. The overseer confided to me that once they arrived at Sagarana they were there to stay. In one case, a group of brothers and their families made several attempts to rejoin kin at the northern post but were brought back on each occasion. In this particular case, several of the female members, who were reluctant to leave their relatives at Sagarana, had informed the overseer. Several smaller family groups did manage to leave by going overland to the headwaters of the Rio Pacaas Novas.

The Evolving System

Between 1967 and 1970, the colony continued to increase in size and complexity. New buildings, machinery, and domesticated animals were brought in. The administration expanded and the Indian population grew rapidly in numbers and heterogeneity. Despite the overseer's efforts, the rigid system of control began to erode.

The Padre's success in raising funds in São Paulo and Europe allowed rapid expansion of the physical facilities. Government funds became available for a new school in 1967 and a kindergarten two years later. The governor of Rondônia donated a sawmill in 1966, but it was never assembled. A more modern one was set up in 1969, but failed to function as it was improperly installed and no one was able to repair it. The most successful mechanical additions were the simplest, such as a small motorized shredder for the preparation of manioc flour, and a manual sugar press.

Despite the sawmill's failure, the Padre still felt that mechanization was the answer. He noted that rice production at Sagarana was limited by a lack of milling facilities: the community's rice was pounded in a large log mortar, with the remainder sent to Guajará Mirim to be milled. To stimulate local production, he purchased a thresher and polisher that could be used by both Indians and civilizados. The colonists at the boca planted a large rice crop in anticipation of the machine's arrival, but the model that was finally acquired was too large and had to be permanently installed at Vila Tosta. It frequently broke down, and saw little use. Rice for local consumption is still hulled by pounding it in wooden mortars.

A similar fate befell another experiment that attempted to process the perennial crop of sugar cane. A sharing arrangement was worked out between the mission and João, a Makuráp, who claimed and was acknowledged by the overseer to be headman of the Queimada. The project would involve the cutting, squeezing, and processing of the cane into a fudge-like substance known as *rapadura*. João was to be responsible for recruiting the labour force. A diesel-powered cane press and large cauldrons were purchased in São Paulo and installed on a cement pad. Six of the men from the Queimada appeared for the first harvest, but after several arduous days of cane harvesting they abandoned João and returned home. When it became clear that João could not command the labour of his kinsmen, the project was scrapped.

The overseer laid the blame for these failures on Indian ignorance, unreliability and resistance. The inevitable conclusion was that the project could only succeed through increased civilizado involvement; the possibility of active Indian participation was discounted as unrealistic. The Padre, frustrated by the lack of progress, was persuaded that the problem could best be resolved by increasing inputs of capital and technology.

In early 1967 he shipped a dozen cattle to the boca. The grassland that had been prepared proved inadequate; the cows escaped into the neighbouring forest and plantations. Nor did Sagarana have an experienced cowhand. Within three months the cattle had succumbed to a series of accidents and illnesses, leading to the project's suspension. Despite this setback the Padre purchased a hundred pigs the following year. A hastily erected enclosure could not contain the pigs, and they escaped into the surrounding fields, wreaking havoc and ruining the crops. Some vanished into the forest; others were shot and provided a welcome change in the bland diet served by the settlement's kitchen. The remaining pigs were eventually rounded up and moved to the island across from the settlement to prevent further damage. There they fell prey to snakes and jaguars.

The mission was also eligible to receive government funds for education and health-care and, in 1967, two local civilizados were hired to open a school and a small dispensary. The teacher had little formal training but had worked with indigenous people through the Rondon Commission, which evaluated the situation of tribal groups in Brazil. The health care worker had previously been employed by the Indian Service at Posto Major Amarante, where he had dealt with the medical problems of recently contacted bands. He built a small house and dispensary on the embankment below the main settlement, and his wife was later hired to coordinate the work of the communal kitchen.

The addition of a teacher and a paramedic complicated the administration of Sagarana by generating competition over authority. Disagreements arose over management of the post and division of its responsibilities. Both the teacher and paramedic were somewhat more conscious of the Indian Service's philosophy of respect for Indian culture and advocated a more gentle paternalism.

Rivalry at the post also reflected differences of opinion within the Prelacy: the paramedic was more closely linked to Padre Roberto (now Bishop Roberto). Dunning (1959:19), who worked in the Canadian north, has noted that status competition in mission posts or trading stations leads to instability and conflict, especialy where there is an uneven number of high-status individuals. In Sagarana each faction sought to recruit Indian support, and some young men were persuaded to establish patron client relationships with civilizados at the post. Aware of the competition for their support, the Pacaa Nova were quick to use it to their own advantage by encouraging gossip and manipulating allegiances.

In August 1970, two lay missionaries from Operação Anchieta (Opan), a Catholic action group, were assigned to the Prelacy of Guajará Mirim. Opan, named after a famous Jesuit missionary of the eighteenth century, was founded in 1969 by the Jesuit mission in Diamantina. Opan missionaries are largely young volunteers who work in pairs and tend to specialize in health and education. These two were sent to Sagarana to organize a kindergarten and to provide some nutritional care for preschool children. Both came from urban, southern Brazil, and were well educated but had no previous experience on the Amazonian frontier. They had a romantic view of Indians and were optimistic about what could be achieved. In Guajará Mirim their sense of mission had been reinforced by the lofty ideals on which the colony had been founded. They expected to find a model settlement based on these ideals and were shocked by Sagarana's harsh regime and social relations. Instead of altruistic mission employees working in harmony with the Indians, they found rigid separations, domination by non-Indians, abuse of power and economic exploitation. Instead of Christian teaching and example, the emphasis was on production and control. Not surprisingly, they were strongly critical of locally recruited staff, and protested vigorously to the Prelacy and to the Padre.

The lay missionaries naively believed that the abuses would end once the situation was brought to light. The Padre brushed their complaints aside, claiming that they did not understand the complexity of problems at the mission. The overseer, who resented their criticism, agreed and argued that the lack of progress in civilizing the Indians was the result of restrictions imposed on him, and of the ignorance and stubbornness of the Pacaa Nova. He rejected the volunteers' suggestions and resisted pressures for change, claiming that a relaxation of discipline would create chaos with which he would be left to cope long after their departure. By the end of 1970, the volunteers and local staff were barely able to tolerate each other.

The increase in staff at the mission also complicated the administration of the settlement and weakened the centralized authoritarian model. It contributed to the erosion of the overseer's power and ushered in an era of greater freedom for the Indian.

As these changes were taking place, the native population continued to increase, especially the numerically dominant named groups. By 1969 the Oro waramciyey formed the largest unit, with 39 members; followed by the Oro mbun from Riberão and the Lage with 26; the Oro nao, Oro eo, and Oro at from Rio Negro with, respectively, 20, 5, and 4; and the Oro nao from Dois Irmãos with 5. In August of that year, a further group of 30 newly contacted Oro mbun from Riberão were resettled at Sagarana by the Indian Service.

Isolation and the relatively small number of Indians at the mission had made the earlier regime possible; the overseer's authority and power and the dominated group's weakness had held it together.

The sheer number and great diversity of kin groups coming from the other posts or the seringal now made it impossible for this administration to continue. Physical facilities were strained; co-residence of unrelated persons produced constant bickering and complaining and on occasion threatened to erupt into violence. Members of smaller kin groups felt especially ill at ease, since they had little support in case of disputes. Many new arrivals had experienced much more comprehensive contact with civilizados than had the Oro waramciyey and Orombun from Riberão. Individuals like Tuji and Paleto, from the Rio Negro, had developed a good measure of self-confidence from frequent contacts with rubber tappers, New Tribes missionaries and government agents, and were unwilling to submit to the inflexible authoritarianism of the overseer. Both were strong individuals and heads of larger extended families, and both had a reputation for independence before coming to Sagarana. They cooperated with the regime of the post only if it suited them. The overseer pressured them to conform but never risked a direct confrontation.

Pacaa Nova acquiescence can only be understood in relation to the factors that weakened their ability to resist and to defend themselves. The early population was recruited from the isolated Oro waramciyey, who had the least experience with outsiders. They had just come into contact a few years before, and had not yet recovered from the shock of the epidemics. Coming from a culture where decision-making rested on some degree of consensus, they were not prepared for the aggression of outsiders. This, combined with their insecurity in an entirely new and foreign context, made them susceptible to the bullying and pressure of the overseer. They initially attemped to evade his persistent demands, but this was difficult in the unfamiliar confines of the boca. Resistence to the regime developed slowly. The women were first to withdraw from the daily work detail, and could not be bullied back. Some men moved out of the settlement to establish small gardens, although initially they still showed up for roll-call. Several family groups sought refuge in the nearby forest for varying periods of time.

Relations With The Outside

The Prelacy's efforts to keep Sagarana isolated failed. Since the dispensary was the only medical facility within several day's canoe travel, it was sought out by the civilizados on both sides of the border. Although a large sign at the mouth of the boca proclaimed the village off-limits, it was impossible to turn away patients who would otherwise have to travel to Guajará Mirim, and who resented the fact that much better facilities were provided for Indians than for them. Further outside contacts were inevitable when the health care worker's relatives settled at the boca and regularly entered the mission.

By far the most significant event for the settlement's future was the marriage of the overseer to a woman on the Bolivian side of the boca.

With the birth of their first child, the new father became increasingly concerned with the welfare of his family and plans for his own future. The old regime, which required the overseer's constant supervision and intensive face-to-face encounters with the Indians, began to deteriorate. The overseer lost touch with the intimate details of the social and personal lives that had previously been so crucial to his development project. By late 1970 the records of labour and production that had been so meticulously kept became mere educated guesses based on earlier records. He no longer had the same influence over the young men, since he spent little time with them. Since he was absent from the settlement more frequently, he hired a local assistant, an older man called Silva, who at one time had been in the employ of Henry Ford's rubber plantation on the Tapajos River. Silva functioned as a foreman, but unlike the rest of the staff, he continued to live at the boca, and provided an important link with the social life there. Pacaa Nova visiting the boca used his house as a base, and for the first time were able to observe the normal functioning of civilizado family life. Encounters between Indians and non-Indians, although still infrequent, increased through the greater participation of Sagarana's staff in the social activities at the boca. Some casual but limited social contact took place on Sundays and holidays, when local Brazilians and Bolivians gathered at the boca to play soccer or participate in local festivities. Only when the teams were short-handed were Indians asked to play in the soccer matches. Soccer had become a popular pastime among the younger men at the mission and they were quite eager to play, but spent most Sundays on the sidelines. Nor were they often invited to join in the celebrations or offered food or drink. Most of the civilizados only showed interest or neighbourliness if it was to their advantage. In the presence of the padres they made a great and obvious show of friendship. Displays of fellowship and hospitality also preceded attempts to initiate some profitable exchange or to strike a good bargain. Normally, the wari who accompanied me to the boca were ignored and left waiting outside the houses. On these occasions, men who in Sagarana acted with poise, confidence and dignity, became insecure and withdrawn. Unprepared and unsure of how to cope with the outside world, they quietly and timidly faded into the background.

The increasing encounters with the people of the boca was advantageous to both sides. For the Indians, it opened up new possibilities for exchange and new channels of information about the dominant society. For the civilizado, it offered opportunities for profitable trade or the hiring of cheap labour. Both sides thus supported the opening up of Sagarana to the outside.

Decentralization

The complexity of new developments in the settlement generated a steady chorus of complaints and accusations from all sides, and it became clear to the Prelacy that central control was no longer practical or manageable. Padre Roberto had for some time been concerned with the overseer's methods, especially the regimentation of the Indians. He persuaded the Padre to allow, and even encourage, the establishment of gardens and dwellings away from the center. This process began in 1970. The staff of the mission realized that such a move also had advantages for them. The overseer assumed that he would be able to retain most of the single young men at the centre and that they would be more amenable to discipline in the absence of older family heads. They would also be less likely to return to traditional ways. The teacher favoured dispersion as long as school attendence remained compulsory. He had always claimed that education would work only if children were removed from the influence of their parents. Attendance initially continued at a high level, and the children of those living outside the centre stayed with relatives or, on occasion, with the teacher. School records in the first year, when I was able to confirm them by personal observation, boasted a participation rate of 80 to 85%. Girls tended to be absent more frequently, since they had to look after their younger siblings. During the dry season when most visiting took place, children were on vacation.

The dispersal was expected to resolve the conflict arising out of the co-residence of unrelated groups, much as had the fission of the pre-contact villages. It would also provide an escape valve for those no longer able to tolerate the overseer's constant interference and harassment.

By the middle of 1970, the nucleus of the mission had become the residential focus of the two largest named groups: the Orombun and Oro waramciyey. Although some of them had small gardens nearby, they chose to live at the centre, which continued to provide meals for both Indians and civilizado staff. The menu was simple, consisting mostly of rice, beans, and occasionally porridge. Fish and meat were no longer readily available, as the region was now severely depleted and, when obtained, were generally consumed by the staff. On two occasions, commercial fishermen who had overcrowded their floating fish cages and suffocated half their catch, brought the dead fish to Sagarana where, since the staff refused to eat them, they were divided among the Indians.

The overseer no longer insisted that food provided by the mission be consumed communally at the barracão. As Indian gardens began to produce, dependence on these rations declined. During the month of July, for which I have detailed records, only half of those at the centre picked up their daily rations. Those who did were mostly men and children, as the women went out regularly on foraging expeditions and consumed much of what they gathered.

All Pacaa Nova spent some time at the centre — to work, trade, use the manioc-processing facilities, visit relatives, or just to be close to the dispensary when one of their group was ill. In the latter part of 1970, during the measles epidemic, everyone moved back into the settlement.

Although the original system of labour could not be maintained within the scattered settlement pattern, the overseer was still able to recruit workers through the promise of food and manufactured goods, especially clothing and steel tools, which continued to be in great demand. So great was the desire for these goods that two Oro nao who lived far from the centre still put in thirty days of work between July 20 and September 15, 1970. There were always some who would move into the main settlement and work steadily for several months to accumulate sufficient credit for a gun, a hammock, or an item of clothing. Despite the Padre's infrequent visits, he insisted on maintaining control over the distribution of manufactured goods. This was a source of irritation and discontent for the Pacaa Nova, who had worked hard for a specific goal and then had to wait for payment.

The days preceding the Padre's visits was a time of feverish activity — finishing artifacts, harvesting cash crops, searching for lost or hidden "money." The exchange itself proceeded in a typically paternalistic fashion. The Padre still knew most of the Indians personally and set prices according to whim. It was not unusual for one person to obtain a hammock for a chicken or two, and another to pay for the same item with scrip representing a hundred days of work. The experience confused the Indians and nullified the purpose of the exchange exercise, which had originally been instituted to familiarize them with the local economic system — the value of labour, produce, and manufactured goods. Since many of the wari were still ignorant of the exchange value of these goods, they made unrealistic requests and were pressured into accepting exchanges decided upon by the overseer or the Padre.

Cutting boards for the Sagarana mission

The long delay between work and reward led to a loss of motivation to work for the mission. By the summer of 1970, the Indians began to trade with the outside, especially with the boca. They preferred to exchange their chickens, beans, artifacts or labour for axes and knives, rather than for pieces of paper that could only be redeemed during the Padre's rare visits. Among the first to engage in outside trade were the Makuráp and Jabotí, who obtained trade goods from ambulant traders along the Guaporé. At the boca, the Pacaa Nova found a market for some of their artifacts and were quick to realize that civilizados were less concerned about the functional quality of bows and arrows, flutes and drums, than with the feather or paint ornamentation. Some of the more innovative men began to copy the decorative Moré, Makuráp, and Jabotí items, since these were more coveted than their own rather unadorned equivalents. The Moré had been particularly successful in developing an artifact trade, and the Pacaa Nova had seen this work when it was brought to Sagarana for the Padre. Trade in handicrafts had the advantage of utilizing existing skills and was least disruptive to subsistence activities.

By 1970, despite all the investment in material and technology, the mission was not yet able to meet its own subsistence needs. Approximately one square kilometer had been cleared around the settlement but much of it had already reverted to secondary growth. About ten hectares were under cultivation: three produced perennial crops of sugar cane and bananas; the rest were planted with rice, sweet manioc (*macaxeira*), maize and beans. The overseer blamed poor crop yields on the indifferrence of the Indians who worked the mission fields, and on their pilfering. For example, he calculated that in 1970 the rice fields should have produce 250 sacks, but only 140 sacks were finally harvested. Of these, the colony's kitchen consumed 120, leaving twenty sacks for seed, and no surplus. How much was stolen is hard to calculate, but the overseer was convinced that the women regularly foraged in the mission fields. To compensate for the shortages of locally grown food, the settlement imported additional supplies (in this case, wheat flour, corn meal, powdered milk and vegetable oil, most of which was donated by the Alliance for Progress and distributed through the Padre's warehouse). In partial payment, the overseer sent small quantities of beans, bananas, sweet potatoes, and dried meat and fish to the Padre's household, to provide some more traditional fare to his Indian labour force.

The Satellites

Most of the members of the other named groups established gardens and residences along the baia. The garden closest to the centre was occupied by Tuji, an Oro mbun, who was married to an Oro nao woman. At the time of contact he had been at the Rio Negro, living with his wife's kin. He planted an extensive area, concentrating on the traditional subsistence crops of maize and sweet manioc. His closest kin were at the centre and visited frequently to claim some of his crop for themselves. In the pre-contact situation they would have reciprocated in kind but this was impossible without gardens, and the wages they received were used to purchase trade goods, which were not generally shared. Although he expressed mild annoyance, Tuji was not able to refuse their persistant requests for food. When I questioned him about it, he merely shrugged his shoulders and said "one has to have a heart."

The next clearing, about a five-minute walk from Tuji's, was occupied by a polygamous family of Oro waram from the Rio Lage. The head of this household, an older man by the name of Eeo, rarely visited the centre except to trade a few sacks of beans or some chickens when the Padre visited. His reluctance to spend much time at the centre was probably related to the fact that the two other men who had come to Sagarana with more than one wife had lost them to younger men. Eeo was economically independent of the mission and continued to pursue a more traditional mix of horticulture, foraging, hunting, and fishing.

Two Oro waramciyey brothers cultivated a garden close to that of Eeo, but did not live on the site. It was occupied part of the time by the parents-in-law of the younger brother.

The last settlement of Pacaa Nova before the Queimada was located about two hours by boat from the centre, and was usually referred to as Paleto's garden. Paleto became the focus of most of the Oro nao, Oro eo, and Oro at, who were by far the youngest and most acculturated of the men at Sagarana. Several of them had worked for some time in Guajará Mirim for the Padre . They were joined in the summer 1970 by Uemtocom, an Oro nao from the Rio Novo, who had lived in the seringal but had lost two children to a measles epidemic that had swept that region. He joined a relative from the Rio Novo who was already living there, and was later joined by José, the new husband of his daughter. José, an Oro eo, already had several close relatives living with Paleto. All of the men spent various periods of time working at Sagarana in 1970, and the younger ones devoted themselves to growing beans to trade with the Padre Medico.

The gardens provided an escape from the constant supervision, demands, and interference of the overseer. Men again went out to hunt and fish. Those without shotguns borrowed them from the mission staff or, on occasion, from me. A few of the older men continued to use bows and arrows and were quite successful, especially in bird-hunting. Whole families participated in harvesting wild fruit or extracting honey from hives that were usually discovered during clearing operations. The garden became the focus of gatherings where discussion could take place and conflicts could be resolved without outside interference. The two major club fights that occurred took place in these satellite settlements.

Traditional religious practices enjoyed a revival. Festivities involving drinking, singing, and dancing once again provided occasions for socializing. Chicha feasts were alternately hosted by the Oro mbun and Oro waramciyey at the centre, and the Oro nao, Oro at, and Oro eo in the gardens. However, the festivities were still limited by the overseer's insistence that they should not interfere with the work schedule. Both drinking feasts were held on Sundays, when maximum numbers could participate.

Interethnic Relations: The Mission

Mission settlements and Indian Service posts represent a special case of inter-ethnic contact, where relations between the dominant society and the ethnic minority are conditioned by the Indian policies of these two types of protective intervention agents. Understanding the system and its evolution at Sagarana requires an examination of the attitudes and interests of the Prelacy, the Padre and the rural population that shares the area with the Indian, and an analysis of the native population's situation under conditions of contact.

Mission activity has been part of Brazilian expansion from the sixteenth century onward. The Prelacy's activities were a continuation of that tradition. The Franciscans accepted pastoral work with the native population as an essential part of their mission. In the 1950s the aggressive missionary campaign of the evangelicals, aimed at the native population, re-awakened Catholic concern and stimulated the rivalry that was ultimately to bring the Padre to Brazil. Although he came too late to cope with the early epidemics, he proved to be the key to the Prelacy's involvement with the Pacaa Nova.

The Padre

During the late 1960s, the Padre's interests began to extend beyond his frontier medical practice and his work at Sagarana. He had purchased a large piece of land on the northern outskirts of Guajará Mirim and had erected a large building complex enclosed by a high wall. Covering almost a whole block, it contained garages, storage sheds, a dispensary, consulting and operating rooms, and a basic shelter for longer term patients. It also included a spacious house, and later, a swimming pool. All of this was surrounded by gardens and included a small zoo where a variety of tropical birds and animals were exhibited. In 1970, the medical facilities were expanded by the addition of a small dental clinic operated by a young Bolivian volunteer dentist. Further expansion would include a small hospital; the Padre was currently involved in a major fund-raising campaign. Although the scope of his medical services expanded, he cut his hours of free consultation from two-and-a-half to one-and-a-half hours, and almost eliminated his services to rural areas. The hospital ship and speedboat that were to bring medical services to the rubber tappers and Indians along the Guaporé and Mamoré rivers stood idle at the dock.

As the holder of several important positions — priest, doctor, entrepreneur, director of an indigenous settlement — and as a man who had important contacts in the military, he had become very influential in the territory. He was one of the few in Guarajá Mirim who were invited to a reception in Pôrto Velho for the president of Brazil. Twice, during the period of this research, he entertained the territorial governor, who was fascinated by his work and intimate acquaintance with "savage" Indians. The Padre knew how to exploit this interest in the exotic, and used the young wari who worked for him to entertain important visitors with their music and dances. After dinner, coffee would be served in the cool patio of his house and Indians would play the hollowed log drum or sing the high-pitched nasal melodies of their people for the guests.

The Padre's preoccupation with his other enterprises and interests left little time for Sagarana. By 1970, his interest in the settlement had clearly waned. His earlier optimism was shattered by the dismal failure of his policies. The gossip and contradictory reports from the mission further discouraged him. To avoid the in-fighting, he began to rely more and more on the overseer and, during his now rare visits, consulted largely with him. In Guajará Mirim he was under increasing pressure from the Prelacy to make changes in the administration of the mission. Quick to anger, he responded to criticism by lashing out at his opponents. He blamed the Prelacy's lack of cooperation for the problems at Sagarana and accused everyone at the post, except the overseer, of attempting to sabotage his plans. The tension was palpable during my two visits to Guajará Mirim during that period. Bishop Roberto visited the project to help with its reorganization, but was frustrated by a combination of local rivalries, by opposition from the overseer, who felt his job was on the line, and by the defensive posture of the Padre, who was not prepared to relinquish control. Although Bishop Roberto was in overall charge of the project, the financing had been provided through campaigns orchestrated by the Padre, who retained control over the disposition of funds.

The mission's importance in fund-raising for other Prelacy projects and the Padre's growing operations in Guajará Mirim became increasingly clear to me, and threw light on some of the more puzzling aspects of the relationship between the Padre and the overseer. Most donations came from the developed world, in this case largely from France and Germany, where the vanishing tribes of Brazil had a special appeal. The Padre devoted much time, effort, and expense in preparing slide presentations for his fund-raising trips, and for this, "naked, savage" Indians were much more effective. Since the Pacaa Nova were acutely aware of Brazilian attitudes toward nudity, they were reluctant to remove their Western attire for such photographic sessions. The Padre left the task of coercion and bribery to his overseer, who took a group of young men into the forest to paint themselves for these pictures. The photographic session earned them a few T-shirts or shorts, but also caused some dissatisfaction and resentment.

Given Sagarana's core role in fund-raising, the Padre's major preoccupation was that the post run smoothly, look orderly and progressive, and appear to be moving in the direction of integration with Brazilian frontier society without being a financial burden. He encouraged the Indians to continue parts of their traditional art culture, as long as this did not conflict with the economic development of the post. His attention during the latter part of my stay at Sagarana centered around the question of economic independence or self-sufficiency. During a meeting with Opan volunteers and the bishop, he said in a moment of anger that all he wanted from Sagarana was production. His concern with the appearances, with having the settlement look good to outsiders whether they be government officials, military personnel, or potential donors, explains his support of the overseer, despite the latter's obvious faults and failures. If nothing else, the overseer could mobilize manpower and exercise sufficient control to temporarily give the mission the image of a progressive dynamic community. The report of the Red Cross mission in 1970, which gave Sagarana high marks, as well as the favourable impressions most visitors took away with them serve as testimonials to the overseer's success.

In his own attitudes and relations with native people, the Padre mixed humanitarian concern with paternalism and romanticism. In his view, Indians were pure, unspoiled children of the forest who had to be protected from the corrupting influence of frontier society. He found many of their customs *bonito* (attractive), and encouraged them. Others, which offended his moral standards, he forbade. He referred to the Indians as *meninos* (children) or *caboclinos* (little caboclos). His definition of them as big children suggests parental affection, but affection tempered by discipline and restraint. His conviction that they are in fact incapable of running their own lives justified the strict supervision at Sagarana, and indicates that the Padre was somewhat sympathetic to the overseer's strict regime. An incident involving some of the young wari who worked for him in Guajará Mirim illustrates his attitude. Several of them had ignored his instructions not to leave the compound and had gone into the city. At a mass held in his private chapel the following Sunday, the Padre lectured them on the evils of disobedience and concluded with the following comment:

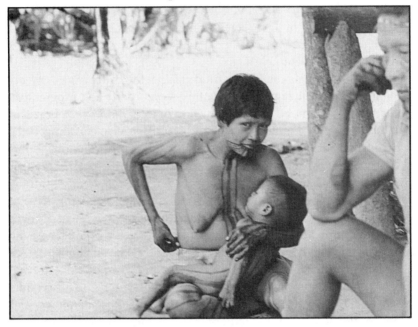

Paint and nudity marked the wari as less than human among the frontier population.

"If you want to go out, you can go back to the woods naked, and live like beasts. After all, you came here to become men."

The attitude suggested by the opposing terms "beasts" and "men" is one that commonly occurs on the frontier. Indians are equated with the wild untamed, and in the process of acculturation become domesticated. Ironically, wild Indians at least command respect through fear; they lose this as they become tame.

In general, the Padre enjoyed playing the role of father. He treated the young wari at Guajará Mirim well, so well that the evangelicals accused him of spoiling them. He took them as a group to the local movie theatre or, on Sundays, loaded them in a truck to go hunting in the surrounding forest. But he had limited time for them and showed little patience with or understanding of their problems.

At Sagarana in the early 1970s, he still revelled in his role as the "great white father," especially when visitors were aboard his hospital ship and he had occasion to impress them with the enthusiastic receptions that greeted his arrival. Since the steady throbbing of the diesel could be heard at least half an hour before the vessel appeared, most of the village was at the dock in anticipation of the Padre and the trade goods he would bring. As the ship slowly inched toward the dock, the Padre in classic paternalistic fashion, threw candy from the upper deck to the waiting crowd.

The Overseer and the Mission Administration

Because the Prelacy's interest in the mission's administration had diminished, the overseer primarily defined the nature of Indian-civilizado relations. Dunning (1959:122) points out that "such individuals represent the Western world and are the primary vehicle for change, but at the same time they are geographically removed from their own social system and its sanctions." They operate more freely, with more power concentrated in their hands. During the early years the power of the overseer was virtually unchecked. Since the Pacaa Nova had been thrust into sudden intensive contact with civilizados, they had not been able to establish institutions, such as that of trade chiefs or captains, to act as intermediaries with the dominant society. The development of conflict among the staff after 1968 reflects rivalry over the power and influence that had previously been in the overseer's hands.

The combination of paternalism and modernization through mechanization that characterized the Padre's approach was applied in Sagarana by an administration that perceived the problem, and its solutions, quite differently. They shared the attitudes that had evolved on the rubber frontier, where maximum control was exercised by a patron over his client, especially if that client belonged to an inferior ethnic group.

The overseer's attitude toward the Indian was one of disdain. He ridiculed their culture, and the smallest deviation from locally accepted conduct called forth censure and reinforced his conviction of their inferiority. He treated respected elders with contempt, often manhandling them or making them the butt of his jokes. He repeatedly scolded the Indians for their ignorance and bestial behaviour in front of other Indians or civilizados; and he mercilessly derided native traditions and delighted in regaling visitors with stories of the Indians' bizarre behaviour. During the measles epidemic in 1970 he joked about their previous cannibalistic practices, saying "that we had better bury the dead quickly before they revert to eating them."

Other staff members were more circumspect in public but shared the same prejudices. On festive occasions at the boca, conversation inevitably turned to the irrationality of Indian behavior, and the locals swapped stories of their experiences with Indians. These anecdotes, some apocryphal, served to reinforce local stereotypes. I was present at innumerable discussions of this nature. When Indians showed "human" traits, such as loyalty or love, the fact was noted with surprise and as a sign that perhaps they were beginning to learn something from their civilizers. Only a few from the boca showed tolerance and sympathy, but not enough to overcome their ethnocentrism and oppose the dominant view.

In the minds of the local administrators and the civilizados of the boca, the Indians were by nature lazy and would whenever possible evade work. The difficulty they had in adjusting to daily labour in the fields or to the steady effort required to operate machinery only proved that contention. The overseer complained that they would get drunk almost daily on chicha if he allowed it. In his view, Indians had to be shown how to work, and constantly prodded to stay with it. He cited those who had established their gardens and houses outside the centre and had reverted to traditional subsistence activities as prime examples; why else would they leave if not to avoid work and engage in "barbaric" practices?

If Indians are lazy, it followed that one ought to pay them less or, if possible, nothing at all. When I suggested paying a guide to take me up the Rio Pacaas Novas, I was discouraged because this would accustom Indians to receive payment for non-productive activities and would encourage laziness.

Although one of the overseer's self-imposed duties was to "civilize" the Pacaa Nova, civilizing them did not mean granting equal status. Indians who presumed to aspire to civilizado status were seen as a threat and were very quickly put in their place. The case of Uemtocom is typical and illustrative. Uemtocom was an Oro nao belonging to the group at Dois Irmãos, which was contacted in 1954-56. Since that time he had worked in the seringal of the Rio Novo and had had little contact with other Pacaa Nova. When his three younger children contracted measles in 1970, he took his whole family to Guajará Mirim for medical treatment. During his stay he was housed at the Centro Medico Social of the Prelacy and was persuaded by the Padre to go to Sagarana where medical care was available, and where he could improve his economic situation.

Uemtocom became quite enthused about the prospect and had all sorts of high expectations of Sagarana. When I saw him in 1970 at Guajará Mirim, he showed none of the reserve and reluctance that characterized the wari at the mission. He spoke in Portuguese and had adopted the civilizado style of greeting, the *abraço* and handshake. In Guajará Mirim, and initially in Sagarana in the presence of civilizados, he spoke Portuguese in public even with his own family. He was optimistic about the possibility of establishing a large garden and raising ducks, chickens and pigs.

At Sagarana, he suffered a series of setbacks. His plans ran counter to those of the overseer, who made it abundantly clear that presumptions and familiarity could not be tolerated and that Indians had "better know their place." Within a short time, a discouraged and bitter Uemtocom moved out of the settlement to the outlying plantations. He no longer made an effort to speak Portuguese and avoided any contact with civilizados. The overseer remarked to me that this happens quite frequently when Indians come from the seringal, or from a longer stay in Guajará Mirim. "They think they are civilized but they soon revert to the old ways." Uemtocom's actions merely served to reinforce the overseer's opinion of the Indian's inability to become civilized.

Indian Reaction

Adjusting to mission life was also difficult for the young men who had worked on the Padre's enterprises in Guajará Mirim and were used to interacting with Brazilians. Pressured by the overseer and by their kin, many were in a quandary, unable to satisfy either side. Those who found wives joined their in-laws despite the overseer's protests. To obtain trade goods, they planted cash crops, especially beans, or worked temporarily at the centre. Those who did not marry found a patron at the centre or, occasionally, the boca, or they participated in full-time wage labour at the mission post. Some were impressed by the wealth and power of the outside world and denied their own culture, but they discovered that there was no place for them in boca society. At best, they might participate in a soccer game and sometimes in local festivities. Some continued to collaborate with the overseer for material rewards, but ultimately most were drawn back into the circle of their kin. A number of these were like Uemtocom, so alienated by this rejection that they withdrew entirely and rarely appeared at the centre.

Their occasional visits to the boca to trade, to watch the civilizados celebrate, or to play soccer provided the Pacaa Nova with the only example of civilizado interaction, community life, and ceremonial activities. It was not unusual to see re-enactments of civilizado behavior back in the village, staged for the enjoyment of those who stayed behind. The entertainment, especially the music and dancing at these festivities, became very popular. Dancing civilizado-style to a record player or an accordian, though infrequent for lack of music, was very much in fashion, especially among the young, and the whole village turned out to watch. This type of communal social activity was encouraged by the volunteers from Opan, who felt that it provided a much-needed social outlet.

The younger wari became keenly aware that the cultural traits that identified them as Indian also singled them out as inferior. Sensitive to public ridicule, they denied knowledge of traditional culture. Uencaremai, who had spent several years in Guajará Mirim and a few years in the village school, adopted that strategy and told me that they had abandoned the old ways when they left the forest: "Things done in the *malocca* (in the pre-contact settlement) are no longer done in the places of the civilizados." He denied that there were still shamans, or that anyone still adhered to food taboos. Most of the villagers feigned ignorance when asked about the traditional social ties, kinship terminology, or ritual practices, shrugging off questions with "*não sei*" (I don't know). Alan Mason, at the Protestant mission of Pitop, found the denial so complete that it seemed they had totally accepted conversion. The younger generation quickly adjusted their responses to what they though outsiders wanted to hear. For example, once they realized that confusion was created by constant name changes of women following the birth of each child, they reverted to using the earlier name when speaking to outsiders. They also began to follow the Brazilian practice of giving the child the name of the father's group. They were aware that civilizados had been quick to seize on such cultural differences as evidence of irrationality and ignorance.

The school at Sagarana encouraged feelings of shame over the traditional culture and promoted civilizado "virtues." In school, the children, all of them Indian, were constantly confronted with the differences between the two cultures. Textbooks used in the states of Amazônia and Pará mentioned the Indian heritage but emphasized the inevitability of change and of integration into the modern industrial world. The role models and ideals taught were those of the larger society, and the teacher stressed that they must overcome the burden of their own culture. The children learned that there was no place for those who did not adhere to the norms and patterns of Brazilian culture. Ironically, the Dia do Índio (Day of the Indian) was celebrated in Sagarana by the administration of the mission.

The most damaging effect of this constant stereotyping and deprecation was that the Indian began to adopt the norms of the dominant group — to accept the stereotypes and to function as if they were statements of fact. Theresa, or Uamcawai, a middle-aged woman from the Rio Negro who had spent some time working in the house of the Padre in Guajará Mirim, told me that if she were to marry again it would be to a civilizado, because *"caboco não presta"* (Indians are worthless). She somehow felt that in my eyes her statement would make her seem more civilized. Loewen (1966:27), who worked among the Chulupi in the Paraguayan Mennonite colonies, documents a similar state of affairs. In response to the question "What is your deepest desire?" he was told, "One wants to become a person." Some wari also accepted the "fact" that their inferiority and the superior knowledge and qualities of civilizados made the latter their natural supervisors and commanders. When I returned to the field in 1972, I spoke to Uruankun, a young man who had been my guide for trips up the Rio Pacaas Novas and who had lived in my house after his wife died, and asked him how things were progressing now that Sagarana was run differently. He told me "not too well, the civilizados do not order the cabocos to work." Chico, a Tupari from the seringal, had the same complaint about the Protestant missionaries at Pitop and on the Rio Negro. "They do not order the wari to work." General acceptance of inferior status is also documented by other authors for various minority groups (Chase Sardi 1973, James 1972, Epstein 1971).

When the Pacaa Nova realized that the frontier hierarchy excluded them, their desire to be a part of that world soured. Many reacted like

Uemtocom, withdrawing and adapting to the new situation by an increased emphasis on their identity as wari or, more generally, as Indians. The establishment of gardens outside the centre facilitated withdrawal and enabled a resurgence of cultural expression.

The basis of this new "tribal" feeling at Sagarana was common oppression, reinforced by a common culture and common contact experience, all of which tended to override named group cultural differences. Toward outsiders, it manifested itself in suspicion, distrust and hostility. Only with some of my closest informants and friends did this hostility disappear. Young people were discouraged from close association with the staff at the post, and criticism forced them to break off any existing relationships. One adolescent girl who had worked for some time in the mission kitchen and had become too friendly with the staff had her clothes torn in reprisal when she failed to respond to criticism. Humiliated, she returned to her kin.

In other Pacaa Nova posts, conversion to Protestantism provided an alternative to Brazilian rejection. By identifying and allying themselves with a subgroup who accepted them as Christians and treated them as brothers and sisters in the faith, the Pacaa Nova evaded the stigma of inferiority. Conversion as a means of entry into Brazilian society has become a tactic of several native groups in the Amazon region, such as the Terêna (Cardoso de Oliveira 1964:135) and some Sharanahua (Siskind 1975:185).

Relations With Other Indian Groups

The Pacaa Nova shared the mission with a group of Makuráp, Jabotí, and Guajurú, remnants of formerly much larger groups who occupied the territory to the south of Sagarana. They had worked as seringueiros for over thirty years, spoke Portuguese and, the men at least, did not exhibit many stereotypic features of Indians. At Sagarana they were free from direct control, having established patron-client ties with the overseer. Relations with the mission were channelled through a "headman," a young Makuráp called João. He was an aggressive man who was known to have killed his Bolivian patron in the seringal.

Because they had greater assurance and more familiarity with civilizado culture, members of this group considered themselves superior to the wari, and were quite offended when they were treated like them. They became incensed once when, on a visit to the centre, they were not seated with civilizados at mealtime, but had their food ladled out like the wari. João complained bitterly to the paramedic, who saw to it that a table was set up for them at the next meal. When I visited his house a few weeks after the incident, João made a special point of demonstrating his level of cultural sophistication: he arranged to have our meal served by his wife, at a table, on an enamelled metal plate, and not only provided a spoon, as was common in the seringal, but a knife and fork as well. He also chided me for not bringing him cigarettes, and declared that "we are already civilized and have the same wants and needs as civilizados."

Throughout 1970, interaction between the Makuráp and Jabotí of the Queimada, and the wari, became more frequent. In July and August of 1970, João hosted a series of chicha feasts that were attended by large numbers of Pacaa Nova. At the feast that I attended, about ninety showed up, and some of the younger men and women participated in the singing and dancing. For several weeks Makuráp-Jabotí-style singing and dancing was quite popular in Sagarana. The two groups also intensified trade relations, especially the exchange of ducks, chickens, dogs, and an occasional pig. Some of the wari who did not have close kin at Sagarana spent time at the Queimada and developed friendships with individuals there. Jamai Humai, an Oro nao from Dois Irmãos, referred to João as "compadre." Several young men sought refuge there after club fights or other conflicts.

In general, despite Makuráp feelings of superiority, social interaction had an easy familiarity and lacked the tensions inherent in Indian-civilizado relations. Communication between them was conducted in Portuguese; the wari were much less reluctant to practice their limited vocabulary in front of these others who also had some difficulty with the language. Civilizado behavior and etiquette observed at the boca and Sagarana were more easily acted out with other native people than at the centre, where there was a much greater risk of ridicule. The only time I ever observed a Pacaa Nova attempting to sing a Brazilian ballad was at the Queimada. The performer, one of the younger Oro nao, had fashioned a primitive banjo out of a flat jam tin, some wood, and a fishing line. He played a quite competent rendition of a Nordestino folk ballad that he had heard in Guajará Mirim while in the employ of the Padre.

The Makuráp Jabotí influenced the wari in a number of ways. They passed on elements of Brazilian culture and patterns of behaviour learned in the seringal; they widened the concept of caboco and demonstrated to the wari that they were not alone, that there were others who shared similar cultural patterns and had to cope with similar problems of adaptation. João recognized this commonality in announcing to a group of visiting Pacaa Nova that "we are all *cabocos brasileiros*" (Brazilian Indians). Other Makuráp had apparently played a similar role in the acculturation of the Tuparí in São Luis in the 1950s (Caspar 1957:289).

The Makuráp Jabotí, although still discriminated against as cabocos, had achieved more satisfactory relations with civilizado society. The overseer did not dare abuse them to the same extent, and they were able to obtain the coveted manufactured goods without being subjected to the missions's tight control. They thus provided an achievable model for the wari to emulate.

The Crisis

In the summer of 1970 an epidemic of measles spread through the areas to the north and down the Mamoré. The colony was closed to outside visitors but, despite this precaution, several wari at Sagarana contracted the illness. It ran its course and the patients seemed to be recovering when two suddenly died. Twenty or more were soon burning with fever. The Padre was alerted and quickly arrived; his visit was limited to a few hours, during which he examined but did not treat the patients. After his departure, casualties mounted daily.

For several weeks the death wail was constantly heard in the village. It began when death seemed near and continued for several days afterwards. Relatives huddled aound the dying or dead and, overcome by grief, risked contamination by placing themselves beneath the body as if to revive it by their warmth. Others, overcome with the shock, became catatonic.

Faced with this mass tragedy, the paramedic was unable to handle the magnitude of the task. Opan volunteers tried to provide some care and comfort, but lacked both the means and the knowledge. At the height of the epidemic, a medical fact-finding mission of the International Red Cross, consisting of three medical doctors and a Swiss anthropologist, flew into the post with the Padre. They stayed for two to three hours, offered no assistance and, after some words of advice to the paramedic, returned to Guajará Mirim. They were clearly more concerned with making a showing and observing the bureaucratic niceties than in the well-being of the post's fever-ridden inhabitants. During their brief visit, I was on the river on my way to Guajará Mirim with a boy who was suffering from a dangerous intestinal ailment. In town, I was briefly introduced to the Red Cross anthropologist, with whom I tried to discuss the situation at the mission. He showed little interest or concern. The official report (Akerren 1970) based on their visit was superficial and full of inaccuracies.

Another eight Pacaa Nova died after the departure of the Red Cross team. By the end of the epidemic, more than twenty had succumbed to the fever and its after-effects. The recently contacted Oro mbun from Riberão were most severely affected. Elementrary precautions and proper care could have prevented this tragedy.

Shortly thereafter, in late July, a serious fire levelled much of Sagarana: several fields in the vicinity of the settlement had just been fired and were still smoldering when strong winds blew sparks onto the roofs of several houses. One landed on the roof of the tool shed where the kerosene supply was kept. It exploded, setting the barracão and several houses ablaze. The central part of the village became an inferno, and it seemed that the whole village would be destroyed. Luckily, the strong winds died down, but when the smoke had cleared the tool shed, the central barracão, the manioc processing shed, and several houses had been reduced to ashes.

These two dramatic events — epidemic and fire — brought the question of Sagarana's future to a head.

Conclusion

The goal of anthropological inquiry is to make sense of social interaction, and in this case to make sense of social and economic relations at the mission of Sagarana, and to relate them to similar conditions of inter-ethnic contact elsewhere.

Missions, Indian Service Posts, reservations, and indigenous parks illustrate the great similarities in the situation and responses of native peoples, despite their diverse cultural backgrounds and contact experiences. What makes for this commonality?

Culture contact from the perspective of acculturation is defined as "a process that occurs when groups having different cultures come into intensive first-hand contact, and results in changes in the original culture patterns of one or both groups." Given this definition, one would expect to find considerably more diversity. Why then do these settlements not exhibit much greater variation? What delimits the choices that native cultures can exercise in a contact situation? An important part of the answer is that after contact with Western society and, in the case of the Pacaa Nova, after pacification, the native society ceases to be politically and in most cases economically independent. As Berkhofer (1965:XI) found in a study of missions in the great plains of North America, "Once autonomy is lost the very nature of contact is determined by the culture in the dominant position."

Following the Pacaa Nova's loss of independence in the 1950s and early 1960s, its relations with the surrounding Brazilian society were structured according to a hierarchical pattern established by the dominant society which, of course, acted in its own interests. The cultural identity and characteristics of the dominant group became the symbols of privilege and power; conversely, the racial and cultural differences of the Indian population symbolized inferiority. In short, acculturation was limited by the nature of the situation of domination. The dominant society perceived itself as a civilizer and set up a rigid code of behavior which, if followed, should lead to the Indian's acceptance into local society; at the same time, that society blocked the goal through a host of discriminating mechanisms that punished those who learned too well. The frontier society manipulated ethnic origin and putative racial differences to maintain these asymmetrical relations, thereby justifying its own racial prejudices and exploitation. The racist attitudes led them to reject Indians as human beings and denied them access to the local society and to any role but that of working for the civilizado.

Old Oro mbun woman with hair shaved in mourning for a son that perished in the Sagarana epidemic of 1970.

Excluded by the dominant society, Indians turned to the familiar patterns of their own culture and to those that shared their situation. Their common predicament and exploitation became the basis of their self-recognition. However, this taking refuge in ethnic identity only served to justify further discrimination, and strengthened the civilizados' belief that the Indian was not capable of change and assimilation. The case of Uemtocom of Sagarana, who was ready to become a Brazilian but was rejected for his presumption, illustrates this very well. He had assumed that if he relinquished the relevant cultural markers, upward mobility would be possible. Price, who worked with the Nambicuara in the nearby state of Mato Grosso, also noted that his most acculturated informants would gladly have disappeared into the Brazilian mainstream, but were denied assimilation by local prejudice (Price, personal communication). The pattern is not limited to Brazil.

Dunning (1959a:181) also reported it in northern Ontario, where Indians saw themselves as snubbed by the dominant society. That this was a common historical pattern is further demonstrated by the work of Berkhofer (1965).

The reaction of Uemtocom was common and perhaps inevitable. Unable to renegotiate his status, he withdrew to the security of his own culture and avoided contact with the outside. It is important to realize that Uemtocom's resumption of ethnic identity is not the result of conservatism or a rejection of outside cultural elements. Rather, it is an adaptation to his inability to enter the dominant society that was his first choice.

The cultural characteristics that Uemtocom or other Pacaa Nova may begin to display, though they reflect primarily their own heritage, may not be the central ones of that heritage or may be borrowed from other higher status ethnic groups such as the Makuráp, who are viewed as having more successfully adjusted to the dominant society. In consequence, together with increasing change in areas of technology and the economy, we may encounter an intensification of the symbols of native culture, leading to greater similarities and to a pan-Indian consciousness as a strategy of opposition.

In North America, greater ethnic consciousness combined with what James (1970:440) calls the "romantic stereotype" has gone hand-in-hand with increasing expertise in business and in dealing with government bureaucracies. The emergence of pan-Indian consciousness as opposed to specific tribal consciousness, has also progressed much further. A similar phenomenon seems to be developing in Brazil, and is being encouraged by pro-Indian organizations such as CIMI, a Catholic missionary organization, and various other indigenist groups.

Among the Pacaa Nova at the Protestant missions, entry into the dominant society has taken place through conversion. Acceptance by the dominant society is limited to the small evangelical community, which justified it in religious terms by the symbol of commonality in Christ.

In the introductory pages I suggested that the concept of internal colonialism was useful in characterizing situations of political control by one ethnic group over another. Such control is accompanied by ethnic discrimination, social inferiority, residential segregation, economic subjugation, and judicial incapacity. In combination, these give colonial relations their particular character and separate them from other types of relationships of subordination, such as class.

In such circumstances the control of the state may be direct or indirect. It may merely deny citizenship to members of the minority group; or it may take a direct role in administering native groups through a government agency such as FUNAI, or delegate power to a mission organization responsible to the agency. According to Roberto Cardoso de Oliveira (1966), control by an "agency of protective intervention" constitutes a specialized form of internal colonialism.

In Brazil, the indigenous people are brought into the national system through a combination of ecological and economic factors, as well as by the threat of force. Once in contact, they are pressured to settle around residentially permanent non-Indians, who can exercise control over them while their territories are occupied by representatives of the expanding economic frontier. Permanent contact puts the native under the restraints of protective intervention policies and under government tutelage. Law #6001, of 1973, does make provisions for release from tutelage and for individual and even community integration, but in the first case only through judicial decision, and in the second, only by presidential decree (FUNAI 1975). Indians are rarely given responsibility for their own administration; the ethnic stereotype prevents this. Legislation, however, is only one aspect of the problem. Unfamiliar with the dominant culture, and with little access to the operational information required to make his way in the new situation, natives are simply unaware of their rights, and are constantly at the mercy of the greedy, the seeker of souls, or the patronizing do-gooder.

Domination is maintained by rigid separation of the two groups. All interaction is conditioned by factors of ethnicity or race, and relationships are what Stymeist (1975:170), in his analysis of similar relations in the Canadian North, refers to as "single stranded." The local members of the dominant society prevent participation in their society by a doctrine of racial inferiority, justified by a negative stereotype of the dominated that defines them from the outset as a failure. In Latin America, the doctrine goes back to colonial times: the idea of innate qualities believed to be associated with different racial groups were embedded in race legislation (Moerner 1967).

In Sagarana's case there were two stereotypes in action. One was reflected in the paternalism of the missionaries and FUNAI, the other in the harsh treatment and exploitation of Indians by the frontier population. The first sees Indians as innocent and immature, the second views them as lazy, drunken, and unreliable. Cardoso de Oliveira reports a similar dual classification that characterizes the Indian as a "big child" or as a "treacherous savage" (1966). In both cases, the Indian is portrayed as lacking something, as incapable. The "big child" image is well represented by the Padre, who sometimes appeared as a tolerant parent, and at other times an exasperated, angry disciplinarian who lectured them on becoming men.

At Sagarana the local stereotype was constantly reinforced by reference to real or imaginary cultural disparities. The most vociferous claims for such differences were made by people who were racially and culturally closest to the dominated; they would go to considerable lengths to point these out and to thereby ensure their own status. It is not unusual that the traits used by the dominant society to characterize the natives are in fact effects of contact and colonization. Excessive drinking, apathy, withdrawal — all are reactions employed by the dominated to deal with outside aggression.

Both stereotypes deny the Pacaa Nova a normal character and real human feelings. Outsiders are astonished to observe demonstrations of love or grief; they are not quite prepared to grant a native the same humanity they grant to members of their own culture. Members of the local population who compete with Indians for access to land and resources have traditionally regarded Indians as closer to beasts than to humans. In one well-publicized incident in Colombia, a group of ranchers were initially acquitted of the murder of forty Cuiva Indians by pleading that, on the frontier, wild Indians were considered to be no different from animals, and could therefore be hunted (Bonilla 1972:66).

The perspective of internal colonialism in the case of the Pacaa Nova in 1970 provides an appropriate model for Indian-Brazilian relations. There is no evidence of any major shift in relationship or in the willingness of the dominant society to accept the Indian on equal terms under present socio-economic conditions. But social relations never remain static; they are constantly influenced by historical events, and opportunities that can modify the situation continually arise for both sides. Cardoso de Oliveira (1968:354) suggests that the model of internal colonialism will start to break down under the impact of rapid economic change, which opens new adaptive possibilities for both Indians and civilizados. Wilson (1970:142) also suggests that upward mobility can take place under situations of economic growth, when members of the dominant society no longer perceive the subordinate group as a threat to their advancement. In such situations the caste-like relations that characterize ethnic interaction will begin to be superceded by class relations, as Indians enter the lower levels of the peasantry and lose their ethnic distinctiveness. Change may also be initiated by pro-native forces within the dominant group. Some of these are working to provide information and outside links for the Indian, which will allow him to make use of the legal system and to engage in political action. Alliances with these members of the dominant society and access to the national press can appeal to forces within the dominant society that find ethnic stratification antagonistic to capitalist virtues and the ideal of upward mobility.

EPILOGUE

On March 23, 1971, the administration of the indigenous settlement of Sagarana was officially transferred to Opan. In addition to one of the 1970 volunteers who had remained, an administrator, a teacher, and a nurse were installed. When I visited the mission in June 1972, the administration had changed again, and a young couple from southern Brazil were now in charge. Among the Pacaa Nova, many familiar faces were missing. A few, like Uruaunkun, were working in Guajará Mirim for the Padre, but others had returned to the north, to Rio Negro and Riberão. The Queimada had divided into two camps and more than half, mostly Jabotí and Guajurú, had returned to Ricardo Franco. Relations between volunteers from other areas of Brazil and the population at the boca were deteriorating rapidly. Mutual mistrust and suspicion led to serious misunderstandings. Neither side was prepared to communicate frankly with the other and the resultant recriminations drove them ever-further apart. Those at the boca who had been more friendly to the Indians were tarnished with the same brush as the more obvious exploiters, and the volunteers often made accusations without verifying all of the relevant information. They accused the civilizados of theft of mission property and illegal trespass. These in turn spread rumours about the mission, especially the loose morals of the volunteers and unfair trading practices. The volunteers accused the locals of abusing the Indians. To the peasants at the boca, the program of the volunteers made no sense — all they could see was the total disorganization of the mission. Since the overseer's departure and the Padre's withdrawal of support, the place was in turmoil. Even some of the younger Indians, like Uruaunkun, commented that things were not progressing well now that the administration no longer ordered the cabocos to work.

The mission itself was completely decentralized. The volunteers lived in the old centre and all the Pacaa Nova were now living at their own gardens. The volunteers encouraged the production of cash crops, especially rice and beans, and stocked a large amount of trade goods to purchase them. When asked about prices, they claimed that the goods were being sold at ten percent above cost. The volunteers, all young people with more enthusiasm than practical experience, had formulated a series of objectives to guide their work with the Indians. They listed their aims in descending order of importance, as economic independence, proper diet, knowledge of the value of commercial products and labour, prevention of assimilation, settled existence, and finally "animating the Indian to explore the natural riches of climate and soil." No mention was made of the land question.

Working at the other posts on the Rio Pacaas Novas were a new breed of FUNAI agents, selected through civil service examinations, well paid and well educated. They had participated in a new three-month training course that included some exposure to anthropology and linguistics. FUNAI encouraged the production of cash crops as well as the extraction of rubber and Brazil nuts. The agent at Rio Negro was also promoting the manufacture of crafts, which FUNAI was now marketing through a series of specialized boutiques in Brazil's major tourist centres. Some of these crafts, especially feather ornaments, led to increased hunting of endangered species such as the macaw. Because the price of a headdress now purchased as many as ten shotgun shells, these birds were being shot whenever possible.

The new Indian agents were still very isolated, with little support from the Agency. At that time, all regional directors were military men who shared their government's overwhelming concern for economic growth, and its view that the exploitation of the Amazon region was important to that development. The agents I spoke to in Pôrto Velho, Guajará Mirim and at the posts had more concern for native welfare, but all shared a rather romantic notion of wild Indians. They expressed a preference for working with Indians in the early process of pacification, like the Cinta Larga, rather than the more prosaic activity of running an established post of peasant-like, tame Indians such as the Makuráp and Jabotí. On visiting a variety of posts, I had the feeling that many agents would not long tolerate the isolation, especially since the local population of rubber tappers were almost as culturally distanced from them as the Indians, and that FUNAI'S new committment to land demarcation would antagonize the peasant population and create additional friction.

This prediction was confirmed in 1977, when I again travelled to Brazil and visited the Pacaa Nova. Along the Guaporé River at Ricardo Franco, the agent was absent and I was told that he spent much of his time in town. The male nurse in charge was completely alienated from the local civilizados. FUNAI'S expropriation of land along the river had resulted in the eviction of the peasants with only three months notice and no compensation, even for families that had lived there for twenty years. In protest, local boats refused to dock at Ricardo Franco, even in cases of emergency. The nurse's only social contacts were with a small group of Makuráp, Canoé, Jabotí, and Tuparí Indians.

Further north, at Sagarana, relations between the Opan administration and the peasants at the boca had reached a new low. Everywhere I went at the boca the new administrator was soundly criticized. The boat of the Prelacy, which at one time had provided some assistance by transporting people and products, now charged dearly. The Opan administrator had apparently made a number of public accusations of theft and had almost come to blows with several of the men at the boca. The mission itself had changed since my last visit. Many Pacaa Nova, including some of the most prominent men such as Paleto and Pancabrem, had left for the post on the Rio Pacaas Novas and Rio Riberão. Virtually all the Oro nao were gone. Opan had introduced sheep, cattle, and some horses, and had purchased a tractor and a few wagons. Life for most wari had changed very little. Most of the older generation practiced a mixed agricultural economy, and grew enough surplus to purchase needed trade goods. Some of the younger men were collaborating with Opan, utilizing the new technology and experimenting with domesticated animals in order to be able to purchase luxuries like radios and record players.

The land issue, probably the most important factor for the survival of the Pacaa Nova as an ethnic entity, had not yet been resolved, but I was told that the concession granted to the Prelacy would be turned over to INCRA (the land reform agency) and FUNAI for distribution. In a map published by Gilio Brunelli (1986:38), a large area stretching north of the boca is shown as Pacaa Nova territory.

The land along the Rio Pacaas Novas had also been demarcated by FUNAI, and the rubber tappers and peasants along the right bank had been evicted. Each Indian settlement had an allocated territory but the parcels were not contiguous. This arbitrary separation was bound to create serious problems, since the Pacaa Nova at the time of contact had intermarried and moved frequently between settlements. The settlement at Rio Negro, for example, had a population of 90 in 1972 and 188 in 1976 as a result of immigration. Families moved in order to be with relatives, to congregate around a popular missionary, or to facilitate their access to trade goods.

Almost all the inhabitants of the Rio Negro area, including those who had moved back from Sagarana, had converted to evangelical Protestantism. The FUNAI agent at the post, the same man I met there in 1972, was one of the few agents who had survived for such a long time in a remote outpost, although he had sent his wife to Guajará Mirim for medical reasons and to ensure the education of his son. He was now requesting a transfer to a position in the more developed part of Brazil. During the last few years at the post, he had converted to fundamentalist Protestantism, and had developed a working relationship with the missionaries.

The missionaries at Rio Negro were a Canadian couple with over ten years of experience and considerable popularity among the Pacaa Nova. They had trained a cadre of catechists, who now conducted the weekly religious services. On Saturday afternoons, the outlying population would filter into the core settlement where the meeting house was located. Saturday was largely taken up by visiting, and by soccer games for children and young adults. The two-hour evening service consisted of Bible reading and hymn singing, and seemed to be well-attended. Morning and evening Sunday services followed a similar pattern, but included discussions of community and inter-community affairs. While I was there, the residents voiced some problems they were having with the occupants of the neighbouring post of Dr. Tanajura. It was clear that the religious service served important inter-and intra-community functions, and led to the voicing of significant economic, political and moral issues.

My most serious concern with the work of the New Tribes missions was that the Pacaa Nova had become too dependent on the missionaries, and in this case on an extraordinary FUNAI agent. They were basically unprepared to deal with the outside in economic and political matters. By 1977, FUNAI had shown that is could not protect the Indians in the face of strong economic pressure, and that Protestant missions were not about to oppose the government, since they feared expulsion from the field.

My general impression of western Rondônia was that of an economic backwater, unrepresentative of the currents that were sweeping most of the vast Amazon territory in the 1970s. Since the beginning of the decade, economic and geopolitical ambitions and a huge and ever-increasing international debt had motivated great infra-structural projects designed to exploit the enormous resources of the Amazon watershed. The flood of people involved in the construction of roads, mines, saw mills, and cattle ranches, were threatening to engulf the remaining tribal remnants. Government-sponsored development had brought great demographic and economic changes to the region, and indigenous policies were continually subordinated to economic considerations. FUNAI is in fact located in the Ministry of the Interior, which is responsible for economic development. Successive FUNAI presidents, many of them military officers, have shared the opinion of Bandeira de Mello that "assistance to the Indian must be as complete as possible but cannot obstruct the development of Amazonia" (Estado de São Paulo: 6,11,72).

The Indian agency has been pushed by economic pressures to develop policies of rapid integration, to allow for immediate occupation and exploitation of the territories inhabited by the last remaining tribal groups. Native people were treated almost as an afterthought during the height of the expansion in the 1970s: for instance, the Indian Service was rarely consulted as the roads were planned, even if those roads crossed indigenous reserves or parks. It has proven very difficult to apply protective legislation, as Taylor's analysis (1981) of the Yanomamo park so aptly illustrates. International pressures finally forced government action, and a unified area was set aside for the Yanomamo, but whether the government will in future prevent the penetration of colonists and mining interests remains to be seen. Apparently, requests for mineral research in Indian territory continue to inundate the Department of Mineral Production. The Department is obliged to consult with FUNAI which, in 1985, had not yet clarified its position on the question (Flavio Pinto 1986:29).

In the middle 1970's Brazil abandoned its strategy of a combination of large scale development and land reform through colonization and entered a new stage of major capital intensive regional development. Amazon expansion focussed on a series of development centres. To finance the necessary infrastructure, Brazil applied to the World Bank and other international lending agencies.

One of these large proposals, the Polonoroeste Project led to the opening of the northwestern Amazon. Intense pressure by social scientists and well organized pro-Indian groups in Brazil and abroad persuaded the World Bank to ask for a commitment by the Brazilian government to demarcate Indian lands within the Project area, guarantee their inviolability, and evict squatters. To this end, anthroplogists were contracted to collect available data on the size and situation of the various tribal groups and, subsequently, to monitor and evaluate the assistencial effort through a regular series of reports. Funds were provided to assist in land titling, education, and health and agricultural improvement. The budget itself was administered by the Indian Service (FUNAI).

It was through such an evaluation that the most recent information was made available to me. A Brazilian anthropologist, Dionéa Braga de Toledo Mancuso, visited the area administered by the Ajudancia de Guajará Mirim in June of 1986, and March and April of 1987, and was kind enough to provide me with a copy of her report. The Ajudancia includes in its jurisdiction all of the Paaca Nova posts and, as of July 1987, it took over the area of Sagarana, which up to that time had been administered through the Prelacy of Guajará Mirim.*

---

* The surveys which form the bases of these reports are by necessity based on relatively short periods of fieldwork. They therefore are biased toward information that is most readily available and from sources that are likely to be most cooperative. They rely more often on comments by administrators who want to talk to anthropologists, natives who are most acculturated, or those who oppose current changes most vociferously and groups with philosophies that they know will appeal to the surveyor. Relatively unrepresented will be the views of older, more conservative native informants, and those who have withdrawn from the posts or settlements, as well as the views of outsiders like the New Tribes missionaries who have consistently received bad press from anthroplogists because of their ethnocentric approach. This latter problem has resulted in a great lack of information on interethnic relations between evangelical missionaries and native societies, an unfortunate situation since these individuals are often the only ones who have any grasp of the native language, and often have extensive knowledge of the culture through their activities in translating the Bible. Both FUNAI and anthropologists are remiss in not making use of their skills and knowledge, as well as their influence over the communities where they work.

The evaluation reports of Dionea Mancuso reflect some of these characteristics. Alan Mason, who worked with the wari in Tanajura, also made a short visit to Sagarana in 1969, and his impressions of the mission show similarities. Both Mancuso and Mason were obviously favourably impressed by the philosophy of the directors of the mission and their approach to the administration of native people, which in contrast to the New Tribes missions and FUNAI, proposes much greater freedom for the Indian to follow his own cultural patterns. Without detailed knowledge of interethnic relations within the community as a whole, one can often be influenced by superficial impressions and good intentions. The report of the mass baptism in 1986 at Sagarana that the author appended is somewhat incongruent with her appraisal, a fact which she herself admits.

It is clear that the situation of Sagarana has improved greatly under the new administration, and undoubtedly under the influence of D. Roberto Gomes de Arruda who since the early years of contact with the Paaca Nova has shown himself to be a champion of Indian rights. The most dramatic religous development in the Sagarana in the 1980s was a mass baptism in 1986. The offical Prelacy description of the conversion is not unlike similar documents produced by the New Tribes, with the exception of greater cultural syncretism in the ritual surrounding the baptism. As I earlier suggested, New Tribes conversion of the groups on the the Rio Pacaas Novas and Lage was a strategy to enter the dominant society and to improve their positon vis-a-vis the local population. In the case of Sagarana this was likely also a factor. In addition, in both cases, members of the mission were clearly liked by many of the wari and it is no inconceivable that the wari asked to be baptised in order to please those who had dealt with them fairly and as equals, in contrast to the local settlers who still see the Pacaa Nova as inferior and who resent the efforts and funds expended upon them. The fact that the request for baptism followed the showing of the video on the life of Christ, with the example of Jesus being baptised by John the Baptist, indicates that some religous pressure was being exerted, despite denials by the Prelacy.

The Sagarana of the mid 1980s seems a more liberal, open and positive Sagarana than that of 1970, with a greater effort being made to integrate the wari into the administration and organization of life at the mission. Wari are employed to teach in the kindergarden, to operate the everyday activities of the dispensary, and to maintain and repair the mission's mechanical devices. The primary teacher who comes from Surprêsa suggested that they might soon be ready to take over the teaching duties at this higher level.

The population of Sagarana has grown to 139, of which 98 are Pacaa Nova. The population is a young one, of which over 50% are under the age of 14. This rapid growth holds true not only for Sagarana, but for the wari as a whole, who have more than doubled in number since 1970. The Oro mbun and Oro waramciyey still make up the bulk of the group. Interestingly, the list attributes the children to the fathers group, a new pattern that was already starting to show in 1970.

Education now includes several sessions a week in the indigenous language and the author notes that young people show a great deal of pride in their native roots and are eager to hear about their culture from their elders, a situation that seems to be encouraged by the present administration of the mission.

The economy of the post is one of mixed agriculture and stockraising. The Prelacy has provided a herd of 270 or so cattle to make up for the steadily deteriorating returns from hunting. The wari plant their own gardens, work communally and provide wage labour for the mission. The author notes that communal work is now initiated by the wari themselves and the proceeds are divided evenly. Why this is so and how it works in actuality is not entirely clear. Wage labour for the community is paid in cash and can be used to purchase goods at the mission at the prices current in Guajará Mirim. The quantity and quality of production is impressive, in contrast to that of the other posts and settlements.

The Prelacy had taken steps to safeguard the land and was preparing to turn over the 10,000 hectares to the wari as soon as legal titles were issued by INCRA, the land reform agency. The bishop had also issued a statement of principles affirming the rights of the indigenous inhabitants to opt for the type of organization that they wished to have.

Increasingly, administrators have taken a positive view of wari culture and let the wari stand on their own feet. Mancuso claims that this freedom has created a new kind of wari different from those at the other settlements who work under the control of FUNAI.

In contrast to the favourable reports on Sagarana, reports of the administration of FUNAI is dismal indeed. Emphasis is entirely on the inefficiencies and almost total chaos at the level of planning and implementation. Many of the problems seem to be symptomatic of a bureaucratic institution that has suddenly been inundated with funds and does not have the personnel, the information or a clear plan on how to administer them. Consequently, both manpower and material is wasted and even the basic and essential job of protecting Indian land from the encroaching settlers is disregarded. Boundary markers and trails are overgrown and settlers enter indigenous areas without being aware of it. Riberão, Lage and Rio Negro Ocaia have been victims of this neglect. Polonoroeste funds for Indian assistance rarely get to the target population and about 80% is used for the administration of FUNAI, effectively strengthening the forces dominating the Indian.

The FUNAI posts are described as badly run, with frequent changes of personnel especially of administrators. Decision-making often falls on those who are incapable, with employees spending much of their time attempting to cover up incompetance. Absenteeism, especially that of the adminstrator, is chronic with decisions constantly being deferred or not made at all.

The indigenous schools, financed by state and Polonoroeste funds, lack proper educational materials and competent teachers who have the experience to work in other cultures. Only the New Tribes missions have bilingual teachers, and FUNAI is concerned that too much time is spent on religious indoctrination and too little on the official curriculum.

Health care, despite some basic facilities in Guajará Mirim and a part-time doctor and dentist, is sporadic and does not deliver the services where they are needed most - in the villages. The Agency's mobile teams only visit the communities occasionally and are usually not accompanied by the part-time doctor or dentist who must maintain their private practices in Guajará Mirim.

Little information is available on the work of the New Tribes missions, which is probably due in large part to their secretiveness and unwillingness to talk to outsiders.

Those concerned with the future of tribal groups felt that the return in 1985 to civilian government in Brazil would open a new and more hopeful chapter for native rights. They were in for a disappointment; in March, 1986, the Interior Ministry, without consulting native people or any of their support groups, passed Decree No. 92.470, which decentralized FUNAI and transferred its major decision-making powers to six regional superintendencies. The decision was particularly ominous because the new regional centres are more subject to regional and state economic pressures, and are in areas where there are no strong, organized opposition groups. The military regime may now be long gone, but the future of tribal groups remains far from secure.

In the late 1980s and early 1990s there has been enormous pressure on Brazil to improve its record in preserving its native peoples and its rain forests — not necessarily in that order. And, not surprisingly, a strong backlash against 'misguided environmentalists' from North America and Europe has surfaced in Brazil. If our attitudes are to prove immune to such criticism, it is essential that we care for people as well as trees; that in doing so we go beyond any romanticizing of the peoples of the upper Amazon as 'noble savages'. More than that, it is essential that we comprehend the complex nature of the changes that their interaction with the dominant culture has wrought — that we are able to offer understanding as well as sympathy for their plight. This book is an attempt to aid in the achievement of those goals.

BIRTH AND DEATHS

1969: 7 births; 2 deaths, both children under one year

1970:

BIRTHS

Date	Name	Sex
May 4	Conjemai	F
May 6	Piro	F
May 15	Uruminkan	F
June 11	Aintot	F
June 22	Pacau	F
August 9	Uruauncrato	M
September 8	Temarauin	M
October 7	Tamcemui	F

DEATHS

Date	Name	Sex	Age	Named Group
April 22	Jap*	F	6 months	Oro nao
May 6	Piro*	F	birth	Oro nao
May 28	Alceni	F	2	Puru Bora
May 30	Uruminkan*	F	15 days	Oro nao
June 8	Machin Tonton	M	40	Oro waram
June 8	Uruminkan	F	19	Oro nao
June 12	Uruau	M	17	Oro mbun
June 17	Pauiam	M	3	Oro mbun
June 17	Uruau	F	10	Oro mbun
June 19	Uruau	F	2	Oro mbun
June 21	Mijei	M	6 months	Oro mbun
June 23	Uijatrim	M	45	Oro mbun
June 23	Pacau*		birth	Oro mbun
June 24	Paton	M	12	Oro mbun
June 24	Uau	F	2	Oro mbun
June 24	Tucupiam	F	2-1/2	Oro mbun
June 24	Tomarai	M	1	Oro mbun
June 25	Piro	F	30	Oro mbun
June 25	Uanhon	M	1-1/2	Oro mbun
June 27	Aintot*	F	16 days	Oro waram
October 22	Mai	F	2	Oro waramcyey

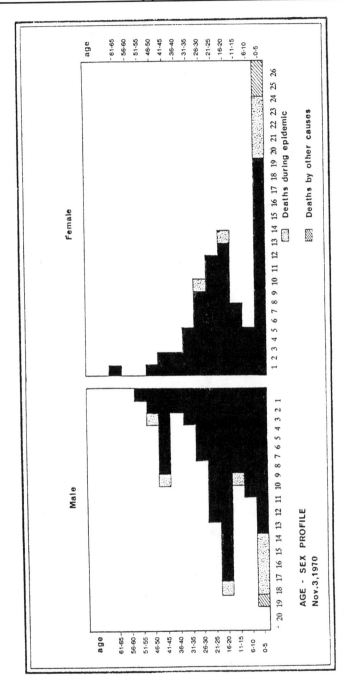

Population Growth — Sagarana main settlement

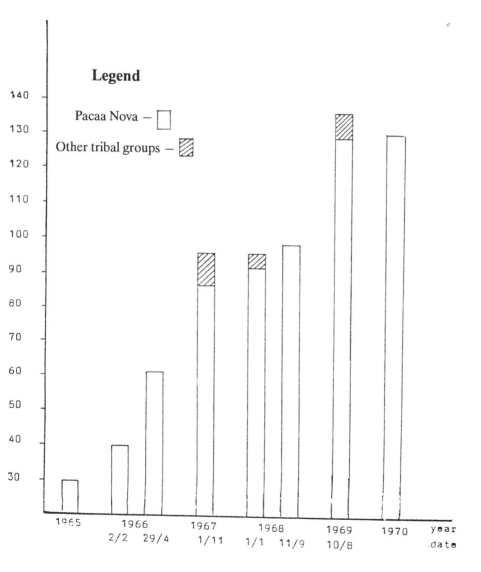

Bibliography

Akerren, B., Sjouke Bakker, and Rolf Habersang
1970 *Report of the ICRC Medical Mission to the Brazilian Amazon Region*, (Geneva: Comte. International de la Croix Rouge.

Ashmead, P.H.
1911 "The Madeira and Mamore Railway," *Bull of the Pan American Union*, 32:432-452.

Baldus, H.
1960 "Antropologia Aplicada do Indígena Brasileiro," *Anhembi*, XL, #119:257-266.

Barbosa de Faria, João
1948 *Glossário geral das tribos silvícolas de Mato Grosso e outras da Amazônia e do norte do Brasil*. Conselho Nacional de Protecão ãos Indios Publicação, No. 76 "Comissão Rondon" Anexo No. 5 Etnografia.

Becker Donner, Etta
1954 "First Report on a Field Trip to the Guaporé Region" (Pacaas Novos). International Congress of Americanists *Anais*, 31:1:107-112.

1955 Notizen uber einige Stämme an den rechten Zuflüssen des Guaporé. Archiv für Völkerkunde X, Wien: 275-343.

1960 Die Wirkung der Zivilisation auf einigen Indianerstämme an den Zuflüssen des Guaporé. Tribus. Veroeffentlichungen des Linden-museums, 197-204. Stuttgart: Museum für Länder und Völkerkunde.

Berkhofer, R.
1965 *Salvation and the Savage: an Analysis of Protestant Missions and the American Indian Response, 1787-1862*. Lexington: University of Kentucky Press.

Bonilla, Victor-Daniel
1972 "The Destruction of the Columbian Indian Groups." In Dostal, Walter, ed. *The Situation of the Indian in South America*. Geneva: World Council of Churches.

Brooks, Edwin, Rene Fuerst, John Hemming, and Francis Huxley
1973 *Tribes of the Amazon Basin in Brazil, 1972: Report for Aborigines Protection Society.* Charles Knight & Co. Ltd.

Brunelli, Gilio
1986 "Warfare in Polonoroeste," *Cultural Survival Quarterly*, 10:2, 37-40.

Bulletin of the Pan American Union
1910 "The Madeira Mamore Railway," 30:31-47.

Burns, E.B.
1965 "Manaus 1910: Portrait of a Boom Town," *Journal of Inter-American Studies*, 7:400-421.

Campos, Murillo de
1964 *O Indio no Brasil: O Problemo de seu ajustamento a communidade nacional.* Rio de Janeiro.

Cardoso de Oliveira, Roberto
1960 *O Processo de Assimilação dos Terena.* Rio de Janeiro: Museu Nacional.

1964 O Índio e o Mundo dos Brancos. A situação dos Tukuna do Alto Solimões. São Paulo: Difusão Europeia do Livro.

1966 "A Noção de 'Colonialismo Interno' na Etnologia." *Tempo Brasileiro*, IV:8:105-112.

1968 "Problemas e hipóteses relativos a fricção interétnica: Sugestões para uma metodologia." *America Indigena*, XXVII: 2:339-388.

1986 "Mining and Indianism in Brazil," *Cultural Survival Quarterly*, 10:1.

Carstens, Peter
1971 "Coercion and Change," in Richard J. Ossenberg, ed., *Canadian Society: Pluralism, Change and Conflict.* Scarborough, Ont., Prentice Hall Canada.

Casanova, Pablo Gonzales
1963 "Sociedad Plural, Colonialismo Interno y Desarollo," *America Latina*, 6:3:15-32.

Caspar, Franz
1956 *Tupari.* London: G. Bell & Sons Ltd.

1957 "Akkulturation bei einem brasilianischen Indianerstamm," *Kölner Zeitschrift für Soziologie und Sozialpsychologie N.F. der Kölner Vierteljahrshefte für Soziologie*, 9:283-309.

Centrewall, Willard R.
1968 "Comment" on Noel Nutels, "Medical Problems of Newly Contacted Indian Groups," in *Biomedical Challenges Presented by the American Indian.* Washington, DC: Pan American Health Organization Advisory Committee on Medical Research, Scientific

Public. l65.

Chase Sardi, Miguel.
1972 "The Present Situation of Indians in Paraguay," in W. Dostal, ed., *The Situation of Indians in South America.* Geneva: World Council of Churches.

Church, George Earl
1875 *Explorations made in the Valley of the River Madeira from 1749-1868.* London: Published for the National Bolivian Navigation Company.

Colby, Benjamin and Pierre Van den Berghe
1970 "Ladino-Indian relationships in the highlands of Chiapas, Mexico," in Van den Berghe, Pierre, *Race and Ethnicity: Essays in Comparative Sociology.* New York: Basic Books.

Craig, Neville B.
1907 *Recollection of an ill-fated expedition to the headwaters of the Madeira River in Brazil.* Philadelphia & London: J.B. Lippincott Company.

Davidson, David M.
1973 "How the Brazilian West was Won: Freelance and State on the Mato Grosso Frontier, 1737-1752," in Alden, Dauril, ed. *Colonial Roots of Modern Brazil: Papers of the Newberry Library Conference.* Berkeley: University of California Press.

Deneven, Wm. M.
1966 "The Aboriginal Cultural Geography of the Llanos de Mojos of Bolivia," *Ibero-Americana*:48.

Dunning, R. W.
1959a *A Social and Economic Change among the Northern Ojibwa.* Toronto: University of Toronto Press.

1959b "Ethnic Relations and the Marginal Man in Canada," *Human Organization*, l8:ll7-122.

Ferreira, Manoel Rodrigues
1961 *Nas Selvas Amazônicas.* São Paulo: Gráfica Biblos.

Fifer, J. Valerie
1966 "Bolivia's Boundary with Brazil'. *Geographical Journal*, CXXXII: 360-372.

1970 "The Empire Builders: A History of the Bolivian Rubber Boom and the Rise of the House of Suarez," *Journal of Latin American Studies*, 2:ll3-146.

Flavio Pinto, Lucio
1986 "Mining permits on Indian lands denounced," *Cultural Survival Quarterly*, 10:1.

Fonseca, João Severiano da
1880 *Viagem o redor do Brasil 1985-1878.* I, Rio de Janeiro 1880; II, Rio de Janeiro 1881

onseca, José Gonçalves da
1875 " Voyage from the City of Gran Para as far as the mouth of the River Madeira," in Church, G.E. (1875) *Explorations made in The Valley of the Madeira from 1749-1868*. London.

'rikel, Protásio
1971 *Dez Años de Aculturação Tiriyó 1960-70—Mudanças e problemas*. Museu Paraense Emilio Goeldi Pub. Avulsas 16.

'UNAI
1975 *Legislação*. Ministerio do Interior, Fundação Nacional do Indio.

;alvão, Eduardo
1959 *Aculturação indígena no Rio Negro*. Bolitim do Museu Paraense Emilio Goeldi (Antropologia), n. 7.

;auld, Charles A.
1964 *The Last Titan*. Stanford University, Institute of Hispanic American and Luso Brazilian Studies.

;rubb, K.G.
1927 *The Lowland Indians of Amazonia; a survey of the location and religious condition of the Indians of Columbia, Venezuela, the Guianas, Ecuador, Peru, Brazil and Bolivia*. London: World Dominion Press.

;uerra, Antonio Teixeira.
1953 "Observações geograficas sôbre o territorio do Guaporé," *Revista Brasileira de Geografia Ano*, XV:2.

leath, Dwight B.
1966 "Ethnohistory of the eastern lowlands of Bolivia." *America Indigena*, 26:143-151.

Iugo, Vitor.
1959 *Desbravadores*, 2 vols. Amazonas: Edição da "Missão Salesiana de Humaita."

ames, Bernard J.
1972 "Continuity and Emergence in Indian Poverty Culture," in Nagler, Mark, *Perspectives on the North American Indians*. Toronto: McClelland and Stewart.

;eller-Leuzinger, Franz
1874 *The Amazon and Madeira Rivers; sketches from the note-book of an explorer*. New York: D. Appleton and Co.

,ange, A
1911 "The Rubber Workers of the Amazon," *Bull. of the American Geographical Society*, XLIII:33-36.

,eigue Castedo, Luis
1957 *El Itenez Selvaje*. La Paz, Bolivia: Ministerio de Educacion Departamento de Ar-

queologia, Etnografia y Folklore.

Leite, Serafim
1938-50 *Historia de Companhia de Jesus no Brasil*. Lisboa: Livrario Portugalia.

Lettre D'Amazonie 1965-1970. Paris.

Lima Figuerêdo, Cel. J.
1945 "Selvícolas do Guaporé," in *Boletim Geográfico ano*, III: 29:731-734.

Loewen, Jacob A
1966 "From Nomadism to Sedentary Agriculture," *America Indígena*, XXVI.

Loukotka, C.
1968 *Classification of South American Indian Languages*, Los Angeles: Latin American Centre, University of California.

Mancuso, Dionéa Braga de Toledo
1986 Relatório. PI Guaporé, PV Deolinda/Sotério, PI Pakaa-Novos—Santo André, PI Pakaa-Novos—Tanajura, PI Rio Negro Ocaia, PI Igarapé Lage, PI Igarapé Riberão. Fundação Instituto de Pesquisas Econômicas.

1987 Avaliação na Administração Regional de Guajará-Mirim e Visita a Área Indígena de Sagarana. Fundação Instituto de Pesquisas Econômicas.

Mason, Alan, W.
1977 *Oronao Social Structure*. Unpublished PhD. Thesis University of California, Davis.

Mason, J.A.
1950 "The Languages of South American Indians," in Steward, Julian, ed., *Handbook of South American Indians*, VI:157-317

Matta, Roberto da
1963 "Notas sôbre o contato e a extinção dos índios Gaviões do médio Rio Tocantins," *Revista do Museu Paulista*, N.S. 14:182-202.

1967 "Grupos Jê do Tocantins," in *Atas do Simpósio sôbre a Biota Amazônica: (Antropologia)*, no. 2:133-143.

1982 *A Divided World: Apinayé social structure*. Cambridge, Mass., Harvard University Press.

Moerner, Magnus
1967 *Race Mixture in the History of Latin America*. Boston: Little, Brown and Company.

Mons, Frederico Lunardi
1939 "De Guajara Mirim a Pôrto Velho." *Reviste Geográfica Americana*, II: 1-21.

Neel, J.V.
1971 "Genetic Aspects of the Ecology of Disease," in Salzano, F., *The Ongoing Evolution of Latin American Populations*. Springfield, Ill., Thomas.

Nordenskiold, Erland
1922 *Indianer und Weisse in Nordostbolivien*. Stuttgart: Strecker und Schroeder Verlag.

1924 *Forschungen und Abenteuer in Südamerika*. Stuttgart: Strecker und Schroeder Verlag.

Nutels, Noel
1968 "Medical Problems of Newly Contacted Indian Groups," in *Biomedical Challenges Presented by the American Indian*. Washington, DC: Pan American Health Organization Sci. Publ.m 165.

Palacios, José Augustin
1875 "Exploration of the Rivers and Lakes of the Beni, Bolivia from, 1844-47," in Church, George Earl, *Explorations made in the Valley of the River Madeira from 1749-1868*. London.

Pearson, Henry C.
1911 *The Rubber Country*. New York: The India Rubber World.

Pinkas, J.
1887 "O Alto Madeira," *Revista da Sodiedade de Geografia do Rio de Janeiro*, III:269-309.

Price, David
1981 "Nambiquara Leadership," *American Journal of Ethnology*, 8:4.

Ray, Arthur
1974 *Indians in the Fur Trade*. Toronto: University of Toronto Press.

Reis, Arthur, Cezar Ferreira
1953 O Seringal e o Seringeiro. Brasil, Rio de Janeiro: Ministério da Agricultura, Serviço de Informação Agrícola.

Ribeiro, Darcy
1970 Os índios e a civilização. Rio de Janeiro: Editora Civilização Brasileira S.A.

Ricardo Franco de Almeida,Serra
1857 "Diario do Rio Madeira 20, VIII, 1790," *Revista Inst. Hist e Geog.*, XX.

Roquette Pinto, E.
1954 *Rondonia*. Wien: Wilhelm Braumuller Verlag.

Schaden, Egon
1969 *Aculturação Indígena*. Livraria Pioneira Editora, Editora da Universidade de São Paulo.

Servico de Proteção aos Indios (SPI)
1955 *Relatorio das actividades do Serviço de Proteção aos Indios durante o ano de 1954.* Rio de Janeiro: Mario, F. Simões ed.

Siolo, Harald
1955 "Eine Masern Epidemie bei den Munduruku Indianern," *Acta Tropica*, 12:38-52.

Siskind, Janet
1975 *To Hunt in the Morning.* New York: Oxford University Press.

Snethlage, E. Heinrich
1937a *Atiko y.* Berlin: Klinkhardt & Biermann Verlag.

Stavenhagen, Rodolfo
1963 "Clases, Colonialismo y Aculturacion. Ensayo sobre un sistema de relaciones inter-etnicas en Mesoamerica," *America Latina*, VI:4:63-104.

Stymeist, David H.
1975 *Ethnics and Indians: Social relations in a North-western Ontario Town.* Toronto: Peter Martin Associates Ltd.

Watson, James B.
1952 *Cayua Culture Change: a Study in Acculturation and Methodology.* American Anthropological Association Memoir 73.